Pentaho for Big Data Analytics

Enhance your knowledge of Big Data and leverage the power of Pentaho to extract its treasures

Manoj R Patil

Feris Thia

[PACKT] open source *

PUBLISHING   community experience distilled

BIRMINGHAM - MUMBAI

Pentaho for Big Data Analytics

First published: November 2013

Production Reference: 1181113

Published by Packt Publishing Ltd.
Livery Place
35 Livery Street
Birmingham B3 2PB, UK.

ISBN 978-1-78328-215-9

www.packtpub.com

Cover Image by Jarek Blaminsky (milak6@wp.pl)

Credits

About the Authors

Manoj R Patil is the Chief Architect in Big Data at Compassites Software Solutions Pvt. Ltd. where he overlooks the overall platform architecture related to Big Data solutions, and he also has a hands-on contribution to some assignments. He has been working in the IT industry for the last 15 years. He started as a programmer and, on the way, acquired skills in architecting and designing solutions, managing projects keeping each stakeholder's interest in mind, and deploying and maintaining the solution on a cloud infrastructure. He has been working on the Pentaho-related stack for the last 5 years, providing solutions while working with employers and as a freelancer as well.

Manoj has extensive experience in JavaEE, MySQL, various frameworks, and Business Intelligence, and is keen to pursue his interest in predictive analysis.

He was also associated with TalentBeat, Inc. and Persistent Systems, and implemented interesting solutions in logistics, data masking, and data-intensive life sciences.

Thank you Packt Publishing for extending this opportunity and guiding us through this process with your extremely co-operative team! I would also like to thank my beloved parents, lovely wife Manasi, and two smart daughters for their never-ending support, which keeps me going. Special thanks to my friend Manish Patel, my CEO Mahesh Baxi for being inspirational in my taking up this project, my co-author Feris for being committed in spite of his busy schedule, reviewers for reading the book and giving meaningful commentary and reviews, and to all those who directly/indirectly helped me with this book.

Finally I would like to extend an extra special thanks to Mahatria Ra for being an everlasting source of energy.

Feris Thia is a founder of PHI-Integration, a Jakarta-based IT consulting company that focuses on data management, data warehousing and Business Intelligence solutions. As a technical consultant, he has spent the last seven years delivering solutions with Pentaho and the Microsoft Business Intelligence platform across various industries, including retail, trading, finance/banking, and telecommunication.

He is also a member and maintainer of two very active local Indonesian discussion groups related to Pentaho (pentaho-id@googlegroups.com) and Microsoft Excel (the BelajarExcel.info Facebook group).

His current activities include research and building software based on Big Data and the data mining platform, that is, Apache Hadoop, R, and Mahout.

He would like to work on a book with a topic on analyzing customer behavior using the Apache Mahout platform.

I'd like to thank my co-author Manoj R Patil, technical reviewers, and all the folks at Packt Publishing, who have given me the chance to write this book and helped me along the way. I'd also like to thank all the members of the Pentaho Indonesia User Group and Excel Indonesia User Group through the years for being my inspiration for the work I've done.

About the Reviewers

Rio Bastian is a happy software developer already working on several IT projects. He is interested in Data Integration, and tuning SQL and Java code. He has also been a Pentaho Business Intelligence trainer for several companies in Indonesia and Malaysia. Rio is currently working as a software developer in PT. Aero Systems Indonesia, a company that focuses on the development of airline customer loyalty programs. It's an IT consultant company specializing in the airline industry. In his spare time, he tries to share his experience in developing software through his personal blog `altanovela.wordpress.com`. You can reach him on Skype (`rio. bastian`) or e-mail him at `altanovela@gmail.com`.

Paritosh H. Chandorkar is a young and dynamic IT professional with more than 11 years of information technology management experience in diverse domains, such as telecom and banking.

He has both strong technical (in Java/JEE) and project management skills. He has expertise in handling large customer engagements. Furthermore, he has expertise in the design and development of very critical projects for clients such as BNP Paribas, Zon TVCabo, and Novell. He is an impressive communicator with strong leadership, coordination, relationship management, analytical, and team management skills. He is comfortable interacting with people across hierarchical levels for ensuring smooth project execution as per client specifications. He is always eager to invest in improving knowledge and skills.

He is currently studying at Manipal University for a full-time M.S. in Software Design and Engineering.

His last designation was Technology Architect at Infosys Ltd.

I would like to thank Manoj R Patil for giving me the opportunity to review this book.

Vikram Takkar is a freelance Business Intelligence and Data Integration professional with nine years of rich, hands-on experience in multiple BI and ETL tools. He has strong expertise in tools such as Talend, Jaspersoft, Pentaho, Big Data-MongoDB, Oracle, and MySQL. He has managed and successfully executed multiple projects in data warehousing and data migration developed for both UNIX and Windows environments.

Apart from this, he is a blogger and publishes articles and videos on open source BI and ETL tools along with supporting technologies. You can visit his blog at www.vikramtakkar.com.

His YouTube channel is www.youtube.com/vtakkar. His Twitter handle is @VikTakkar. You can also follow him on his blog at www.vikramtakkar.com.

www.PacktPub.com

Support files, eBooks, discount offers and more

You might want to visit www.PacktPub.com for support files and downloads related to your book.

Did you know that Packt offers eBook versions of every book published, with PDF and ePub files available? You can upgrade to the eBook version at www.PacktPub.com and as a print book customer, you are entitled to a discount on the eBook copy. Get in touch with us at service@packtpub.com for more details.

At www.PacktPub.com, you can also read a collection of free technical articles, sign up for a range of free newsletters and receive exclusive discounts and offers on Packt books and eBooks.

http://PacktLib.PacktPub.com

Do you need instant solutions to your IT questions? PacktLib is Packt's online digital book library. Here, you can access, read and search across Packt's entire library of books.

Why Subscribe?
- Fully searchable across every book published by Packt
- Copy and paste, print and bookmark content
- On demand and accessible via web browser

Free Access for Packt account holders

If you have an account with Packt at www.PacktPub.com, you can use this to access PacktLib today and view nine entirely free books. Simply use your login credentials for immediate access.

Table of Contents

Preface

Welcome to *Pentaho for Big Data Analytics*! There are three distinct terms here: **Pentaho**, **Big Data**, and **Analytics**.

Pentaho is one of the most powerful open source Business Intelligence (BI) platforms available today on the enterprise application market. Pentaho has everything needed for all the stages, from a data preparation stage to a data visualization stage. And recently, it gained more attention as it can work with Big Data. The biggest advantage of Pentaho over its peers is its recent launch, the **Adaptive Big Data Layer**.

One of the drawbacks of Pentaho is that when you need to customize it further, it requires a steep learning curve; this is what most Pentaho implementers are facing. It is understandable that to use a complex software such as Business Intelligence, you need to have an understanding of data modeling concepts such as star schema or data fault, how to further mapping or configurations that suit your client's needs, and also the understanding of the possibilities of customization.

Big Data is becoming one of the most important technology trends in the digital world, and has the potential to change the way organizations use data to enhance user experience and transform their business models. So how does a company go about maintaining Big Data with cheaper hardware? What does it mean to transform a massive amount of data into meaningful knowledge?

This book will provide you with an understanding of what comprises Pentaho, what it can do, and how you can get on to working with Pentaho in three key areas: a Pentaho core application, Pentaho visualizations, and working with Big Data (using Hadoop).

Also, it will provide you with insights on how technology transitions in software, hardware, and analytics can be done very easily using Pentaho — the leading industry in open source stack. This book will mainly talk about the ways to perform analytics and visualize those analytics in various charts so that the results can be shared across different channels.

What this book covers

Chapter 1, The Rise of Pentaho Analytics along with Big Data, serves as a quick overview of the Pentaho tools and its history around BI Space, weaving in stories on the rise of Big Data.

Chapter 2, Setting Up the Ground, gives a quick installation reference for users who are new to the Pentaho BI platform. Topics covered in this chapter are installation of the Pentaho BI Server, configuration of the server, and running it for the first time.

Chapter 3, Churning Big Data with Pentaho, introduces Hadoop as the Big Data platform, shows you how to set it up through a local installation and a cloud-based installation, and tells you how it's used with Pentaho.

Chapter 4, Pentaho Business Analytics Tools, provides a way to distinguish a signal from noise. You will get familiar with various design tools that will help you to build amazing dashboards and set up reports with the help of the data analytics capability.

Chapter 5, Visualization of Big Data, discusses the various visualization tools available in Pentaho. It talks about Pentaho Instaview, which helps data scientists/analysts to move from data to analytics in just three steps.

Appendix A, Big Data Sets, discusses data preparation with one sample illustration from stock exchange data.

Appendix B, Hadoop Setup, takes you through the configuration of the third-party Hadoop distribution, Hortonworks, which is used throughout the book for various examples.

What you need for this book

You will need Windows 7/8 and a Hadoop instance. This will be discussed in detail in *Chapter 2, Setting Up the Ground*.

Who this book is for

If you are a Big Data enthusiast, a Hadoop programmer, or a developer working in the BI domain who is aware of Hadoop or the Pentaho tools and want to try out creating a solution in the Big Data space, this is the book for you.

Conventions

In this book, you will find a number of styles of text that distinguish between different kinds of information. Here are some examples of these styles, and an explanation of their meaning.

Code words in text, database table names, folder names, filenames, file extensions, pathnames, dummy URLs, user input, and Twitter handles are shown as follows: "Pentaho Report Designer consists of a reporting engine at its core, which accepts a .ppt template to process the report."

A block of code is set as follows:

```
ResultSet res = stmt.executeQuery(sql);
while (res.next()) {
  get(Fields.Out, "period").setValue(rowd, res.getString(3)
  + "-" + res.getString(4));
  get(Fields.Out, "stock_price_close").setValue(rowd,
  res.getDouble(1));
  putRow(data.outputRowMeta, rowd);
}
```

Any command-line input or output is written as follows:

```
java -cp [BISERVER]\data\lib\hsqldb-1.8.0.jar org.hsqldb.util.
DatabaseManagerSwing
```

New terms and **important words** are shown in bold. Words that you see on the screen, in menus or dialog boxes for example, appear in the text like this: "clicking the **Next** button moves you to the next screen".

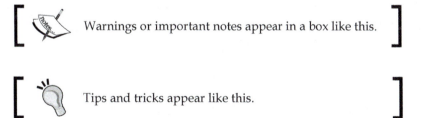

Warnings or important notes appear in a box like this.

Tips and tricks appear like this.

Reader feedback

Feedback from our readers is always welcome. Let us know what you think about this book—what you liked or may have disliked. Reader feedback is important for us to develop titles that you really get the most out of.

To send us general feedback, simply send an e-mail to feedback@packtpub.com, and mention the book title via the subject of your message.

If there is a topic that you have expertise in and you are interested in either writing or contributing to a book, see our author guide on www.packtpub.com/authors.

Customer support

Now that you are the proud owner of a Packt book, we have a number of things to help you to get the most from your purchase.

Downloading the example code

You can download the example code files for all Packt books you have purchased from your account at http://www.packtpub.com. If you purchased this book elsewhere, you can visit http://www.packtpub.com/support and register to have the files e-mailed directly to you.

Errata

Although we have taken every care to ensure the accuracy of our content, mistakes do happen. If you find a mistake in one of our books—maybe a mistake in the text or the code—we would be grateful if you would report this to us. By doing so, you can save other readers from frustration and help us improve subsequent versions of this book. If you find any errata, please report them by visiting http://www.packtpub.com/submit-errata, selecting your book, clicking on the **errata submission form** link, and entering the details of your errata. Once your errata are verified, your submission will be accepted and the errata will be uploaded on our website, or added to any list of existing errata, under the Errata section of that title. Any existing errata can be viewed by selecting your title from http://www.packtpub.com/support.

Piracy

Piracy of copyright material on the Internet is an ongoing problem across all media. At Packt, we take the protection of our copyright and licenses very seriously. If you come across any illegal copies of our works, in any form, on the Internet, please provide us with the location address or website name immediately so that we can pursue a remedy.

Please contact us at copyright@packtpub.com with a link to the suspected pirated material.

We appreciate your help in protecting our authors, and our ability to bring you valuable content.

Questions

You can contact us at questions@packtpub.com if you are having a problem with any aspect of the book, and we will do our best to address it.

1
The Rise of Pentaho Analytics along with Big Data

Pentaho, headquartered in Orlando, has a team of BI veterans with an excellent track record. In fact, Pentaho is the first commercial open source BI platform, which became popular quickly because of its seamless integration with many third-party software. It can comfortably talk to data sources: MongoDB, OLAP tools: Palo, or Big Data frameworks: Hadoop and Hive.

The Pentaho brand has been built up over the last 9 years to help unify and manage a suite of open source projects that provide alternatives to proprietary software BI vendors. Just to name, a few open source projects are Kettle, Mondrian, Weka, and JFreeReport. This unification helped to grow Pentaho's community and provided a centralized place. Pentaho claims that its community stands somewhere between 8,000 and 10,000 members strong, a fact that aids its ability to stay afloat offering just technical support, management services, and product enhancements for its growing list of enterprise BI users. In fact, this is how Pentaho mainly generates revenue for its growth.

For research and innovation, Pentaho has its "think tank", named Pentaho Labs, to innovate the breakthrough of Big Data-driven technologies in areas such as predictive and real-time analysis.

The core of business intelligence domain is always the underlined data. In fact, 70 years ago, they encountered the first attempt to quantify the growth rate of volume of data as "information explosion". This term first was used in 1941, according to Oxford English Dictionary. By 2010, this industrial revolution of data gained full momentum fueled by social media sites, and then scientists and computer engineers coined a new term for this phenomenon, "Big Data". Big Data is a collection of data sets, so large and complex that it becomes difficult to process with conventional database management tools. The challenges include capture, curation, storage, search, sharing, transfer, analysis, and visualization. As of 2012, the limits on the size of data sets that are feasible to process in a reasonable amount of time was in the order of exabytes (1 billion gigabytes) of data.

Data sets grow in size partly because they are increasingly being gathered by ubiquitous information-sensing mobile devices, aerial sensory technologies, digital cameras, software logs, microphones, RFID readers, and so on, apart from scientific research data such as micro-array analysis. One EMC-sponsored IDC study projected nearly 45-fold annual data growth by 2020!

So with the pressing need for software to store this variety of huge data, Hadoop was born. To analyze this huge data, the industry needed an easily manageable, commercially viable solution, which integrates with these Big Data software. Pentaho has come up with a perfect suite of software to address all the challenges posed by Big Data.

Pentaho BI Suite – components

Pentaho is a trailblazer when it comes to business intelligence and analysis, offering a full suite of capabilities for the **ETL** (**Extract**, **Transform**, and **Load**) processes, data discovery, predictive analysis, and powerful visualization. It has the flexibility of deploying on premise, in cloud, or can be embedded in custom applications.

Pentaho is a provider of a Big Data analytics solution that spans data integration, interactive data visualization, and predictive analytics. As depicted in the following diagram, this platform contains multiple components, which are divided into three layers: data, server, and presentation:

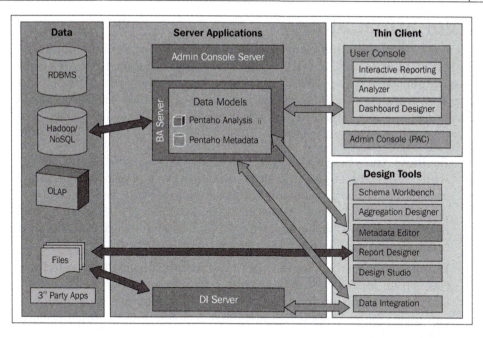

Let us take a detailed look at each of the components in the previous diagram.

Data

This is one of the biggest advantages of Pentaho; that it integrates with multiple data sources seamlessly. In fact, Pentaho Data Integration 4.4 Community Edition (referred as CE hereafter) supports 44 open source and proprietary databases, flat files, spreadsheets, and more out of box third-party software. Pentaho introduced Adaptive Big Data Layer as part of the Pentaho Data Integration engine to support the evolution of the Big Data stores. This layer accelerates access and integration to the latest version and capabilities of the Big Data stores. It natively supports third-party Hadoop distributions from MapR, Cloudera, Hortonworks, as well as popular NoSQL databases such as Cassandra and MongoDB. These new Pentaho Big Data initiatives bring greater adaptability, abstraction from change, and increased competitive advantage to companies facing the never-ceasing evolution of the Big Data ecosystem. Pentaho also supports analytic databases such as Greenplum and Vertica.

Server applications

The **Pentaho Administration Console (PAC)** server in CE or **Pentaho Enterprise Console (PEC)** server in EE (Enterprise Edition) is a web interface used to create, view, schedule, and apply permissions to reports and dashboards. It also provides an easy way to manage security, scheduling, and configuration for the Business Application Server and Data Integration Server along with repository management. The server applications are as follows:

- **Business Analytics (BA) Server**: This is a Java-based BI platform with a report management system and lightweight process-flow engine. This platform also provides an HTML5-based web interface for creating, scheduling, and sharing various artifacts of BI such as interactive reporting, data analysis, and a custom dashboard. In CE, we have a parallel application called Business Intelligence (BI) Server.

- **Data Integration (DI) Server**: This is a commercially available enterprise class server for the ETL processes and Data Integration. It helps to execute ETL and Data Integration jobs smoothly. It also provides scheduling to automate jobs and supports content management with the help of revision history and security integration.

Thin Client Tools

The Thin Client Tools all run inside **Pentaho User Console (PUC)** in a web browser (such as Internet Explorer, Chrome, or Firefox). Let's have a look at each of the tools:

- **Pentaho Interactive Reporting**: This is a "What You See is What You Get" (WYSIWYG) type of design interface used to build simple and ad hoc reports on the fly without having to rely on IT support. Any business user can design reports using the drag-and-drop feature by connecting to the desired data source and then do rich formatting or use the existing templates.

- **Pentaho Analyzer**: This provides an advanced web-based, multiple browser- supported OLAP viewer with support for drag-and-drop. It is an intuitive analytical visualization application with the capability to filter and drill down further into business information data, which is stored in its own Pentaho Analysis (Mondrian) data source. You can also perform other activities such as sorting, creating derived measures, and chart visualization.

- **Pentaho Dashboard Designer** (EE): This is a commercial plugin that allows users to create dashboards with great usability. Dashboards can contain a centralized view of key performance indicators (KPI) and other business data movement, dynamic filter controls with customizable layout and themes.

Design tools

Let's take a quick look at each of these tools:

- **Schema Workbench**: This is a **Graphical User Interface (GUI)** for designing Rolap cubes for Pentaho Analysis (Mondrian). It also provides the capability of data exploration and analysis for end BI users without having to understand the **MultiDimensional eXpressions (MDX)** language.

- **Aggregation Designer**: This is based on Pentaho Analysis (Mondrian) schema files in XML and the database with the underlying tables described by the schema XML to generate pre-calculated, pre-aggregated answers, which improve the performance of analysis work and MDX queries executed against Mondrian to a great extent.

- **Metadata Editor**: This is a tool used to create logical business models and acts as an abstraction layer from the underlying physical data layer. The resulting metadata mappings are used by Pentaho's Interactive Reporting (the community-based Saiku Reporting), to create reports within the BA Server without any other external desktop application.

- **Report Designer**: This is a banded report designing tool with a rich GUI, which can also contain sub-reports, charts, and graphs. It can query and use data from a range of data sources from text files to RDBMS to Big Data, which addresses the requirements of financial, operational, and production reporting. Even standalone reports can be executed from the user console or used within a dashboard. Pentaho Report Designer consists of a reporting engine at its core, which accepts a `.ppt` template to process reports. This file is in a ZIP format with XML resources to define the report design.

- **Data Integration**: This is also known as "Kettle", and consists of a core integration (ETL) engine and GUI application that allows the user to design Data Integration jobs and transformations. It also supports distributed deployment on the cluster or cloud environment as well as on single node computers. It has an adaptive Big Data layer, which supports different Big Data stores by insulating Hadoop, so that you only need to focus on analysis without bothering much about modification of the Big Data stores.

- **Design Studio**: This is an Eclipse-based application and plugin, facilitating to create business process flow with a special XML script to define action sequences called `xactions` and other forms of automation in the platform. Action sequences define a lightweight, result-oriented business flow within the Pentaho BA Server.

Edge over competitors

What makes Pentaho unique to other existing BI solutions is the vast data connectivity provided by the Pentaho abstraction layer. This makes it a very complete solution for data integration across many heterogonous entry systems and storages.

Pentaho's OLAP solution also provides flexibility on various relational database engines, regardless of whether it is a proprietary database or open source.

The big benefit of Pentaho is its clear vision in adapting Big Data sources and NoSQL solutions, which is more and more accepted in enterprises across the world.

Apache Hadoop has become increasingly popular, and with it, the growing features of Pentaho have proven themselves able to catch up with it. Once you have the Hadoop platform, you can use Pentaho to put or read data in **HDFS (Hadoop Distribution File System)** format and also orchestrate a map-reduced process in Hadoop clusters with an easy-to-use GUI designer.

Pentaho has also emphasized visualization, the key ingredient of any analytic platform. Their recent acquisition of the Portugal-based business analytic solution company, Webdetails, clearly shows this. Webdetails brought on board a fantastic set of UI-based community tools (known as CTools) such as **Community Dashboard Framework (CDF)**, and **Community Data Access (CDA)**.

Summary

We took a look at the Pentaho Business Analytics platform with its key ingredients. We have also discussed various client tools and design tools with their respective features.

In the next chapter, we will see how to prepare a Pentaho BI environment on your machine, which will help in executing some hands-on assignments.

2
Setting Up the Ground

We studied the Pentaho platform along with its tools in the previous chapter. This chapter will now serve up a basic technical setup and walkthrough that can serve as our grounding in using and extending Pentaho effectively.

Pentaho BI Server and the development platform

As we learned earlier in *Chapter 1*, *The Rise of Pentaho Analytics along with Big Data*, Pentaho has a community-equivalent of the BA Server application, that is, the BI Server. The BI Server includes the following two web-based applications:

- **Pentaho User Console (PUC)**: This is part of the portal that interacts directly with the end user

- **Pentaho Administration Console (PAC)**: This serves as an administration hub that gives the system and database administrator greater control of the server's configuration, management, and security

The deployment and configuration difference between **Pentaho Enterprise Edition (EE)** and **Pentaho Community Edition (CE)** lies in the ease of installation.

In Pentaho EE, you will have an installation script that eases the setting up of the application. In Pentaho CE, you will have to do everything manually from extracting, starting, stopping, and configuring the application.

This book will focus on Pentaho CE, but you can switch to EE easily once you get familiar with CE.

Prerequisites/system requirements

The following are the system requirements:

- Minimum RAM of 4 GB
- Java Runtime or Java Development Kit version 1.5 and above
- 15 GB of free space available
- An available Internet connection in order to configure and set up additional applications via **Pentaho Marketplace**, a service that is accessible within the PUC

Obtaining Pentaho BI Server (Community Edition)

The following steps will walk you through the task of acquiring your copy of Pentaho BI Server CE:

1. Visit the Pentaho open source project at `http://sourceforge.net/projects/pentaho/`.

2. Click on **Files** as shown in the following screenshot:

3. Click on **Business Intelligence Server**.

4. There are several versions available to be downloaded (as shown in the following screenshot). Choose the latest stable version. At the time of writing, the latest stable version was 4.8.0.

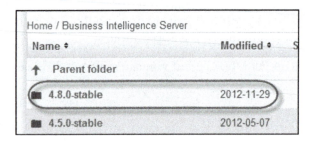

5. If you are using Windows, choose `biserver-ce-4.8.0-stable.zip`. But if you are using UNIX or Linux, you should choose the `biserver-ce-4.8.0-stable.tar.gz` file.

Name ▼	Modified ▼	Size ▼
↑ Parent folder		
biserver-manual-ce-4.8.0-stable.zip	2012-11-28	421.5 MB
biserver-ce-4.8.0-stable.zip	2012-11-28	451.8 MB
biserver-ce-4.8.0-stable.tar.gz	2012-11-28	445.6 MB
bi-platform-4.8.0-stable-sources.zip	2012-11-28	1.9 MB
biserver-ce-4.8.0-stable-javadoc.zip	2012-11-28	6.2 MB

6. Extract the file into a location of your choosing, for example, `C:\Pentaho`. You will have two extracted folders, `biserver-ce` and `administration-console`. We will refer to the folders by `[BISERVER]` and `[PAC]` respectively.

The JAVA_HOME and JRE_HOME environment variables

The BI Server is written on the Java platform, and for the BI Server to work properly, you need to make sure that the **JAVA_HOME** or **JRE_HOME** environment variable has been set up properly. Follow the given steps:

1. Set the `JAVA_HOME` variable pointing to your JDK installation folder, for example, `C:\Program Files\Java\jdk1.6.0_45`.

2. Set the `JRE_HOME` variable pointing to your JRE installation folder, for example, `C:\Program Files\Java\jre6`.

For example, if you set the JAVA_HOME variable in the Windows 7 environment, the **Environment Variables** dialog will look like the following screenshot:

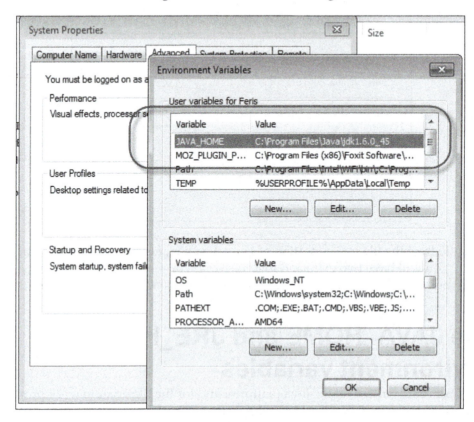

Running Pentaho BI Server

Follow the given steps to run the Pentaho BI Server:

1. Execute the startup script, [BISERVER]/start-pentaho.bat (Windows), or [BISERVER]/start-pentaho.sh (UNIX/Linux).

2. When the script runs for the first time, a **Version Checker Warning** dialog appears. Click on the **OK** button to continue.

3. If you get a `Server startup in [number] ms` message in your console, it means that the BI Server has been started as shown in the following screenshot:

```
Tomcat                                                          _  □  ✕
20:53:04,850 WARN  [PackageManager] Unresolved dependency for package: org.penta
ho.reporting.engine.classic.extensions.datasources.cda.CdaModule
20:53:04,879 WARN  [PackageSorter] A dependent module was not found in the list
of known modules.
20:53:11,105 WARN  [DefaultSchemaGenerator] We don't support method overloading.
 Ignoring [public java.lang.String serializeModels(org.pentaho.metadata.model.Do
main,java.lang.String,boolean) throws java.lang.Exception]
Pentaho BI Platform server is ready. (Pentaho Platform Engine Core 4.8.0-stable.
51169) Fully Qualified Server Url = http://localhost:8080/pentaho/, Solution Pat
h = D:\BI Server\biserver-ce-4.8.0-stable\biserver-ce\pentaho-solutions
Aug 4, 2013 8:53:11 PM org.apache.catalina.startup.HostConfig deployDirectory
INFO: Deploying web application directory pentaho-style
Aug 4, 2013 8:53:11 PM org.apache.catalina.startup.HostConfig deployDirectory
INFO: Deploying web application directory ROOT
Aug 4, 2013 8:53:11 PM org.apache.catalina.startup.HostConfig deployDirectory
INFO: Deploying web application directory sw-style
Aug 4, 2013 8:53:11 PM org.apache.coyote.http11.Http11Protocol start
INFO: Starting Coyote HTTP/1.1 on http-8080
Aug 4, 2013 8:53:11 PM org.apache.jk.common.ChannelSocket init
INFO: JK: ajp13 listening on /0.0.0.0:8009
Aug 4, 2013 8:53:11 PM org.apache.jk.server.JkMain start
INFO: Jk running ID=0 time=0/29  config=null
Aug 4, 2013 8:53:11 PM org.apache.catalina.startup.Catalina start
INFO: Server startup in 21831 ms
```

Sometimes this process doesn't work. The most common problem is the insufficiency of RAM. If you are sure the minimum requirements discussed have been met, and you still encounter this problem, try to close some of your applications.

 The default server port is `8080`, which can be changed from `[BISERVER]/tomcat/conf/server.xml` by changing the `Connector` port.

Pentaho User Console (PUC)

Follow the given steps to log in and use Pentaho User Console for the first time:

1. Open your web browser—Internet Explorer, Google Chrome, or Mozilla Firefox is recommended.

2. In the address bar, type `http://localhost:8080` to access the Pentaho User Console (PUC). A login page appears as shown in the following screenshot:

3. Log in using the default username/password that comes with Pentaho: `joe`/`password`. Click on the **Evaluation Login** link to see other demo users. This link can be removed later when you want to use the application in a production environment.

4. After a successful login, you will be redirected to the PUC working space. Its layout comprises of **Main Toolbar**, **Main Menu Bar**, **Logo Panel**, and **Launch Page**. The following screenshot shows the Pentaho User Console:

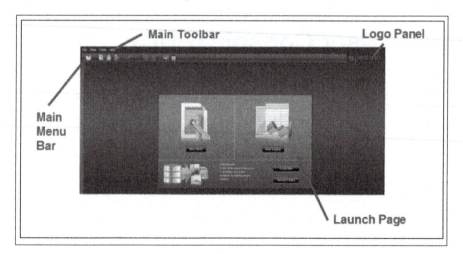

5. In the **View** menu, choose **Browser** to show the **Browse** pane/side pane.

6. The **Browse** pane is divided into two parts. The upper pane is a **Repository Browser** that will show you the solution folders. The lower part will list all the solutions that are part of a selected solution folder. The following screenshot shows the **Browse** pane:

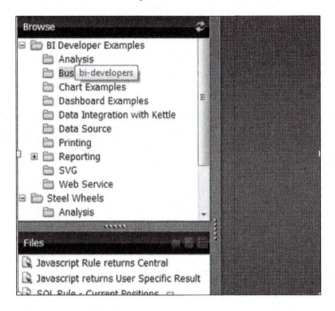

Pentaho Action Sequence and solution

Pentaho **Action Sequence** is an XML file, which defines a *workflow* of tasks in Pentaho. It is needed to glue together several different Pentaho components that need to interact to achieve a purpose such as creating and e-mailing a report in PDF format. For more information on a complete list of components in the Pentaho Action Sequence, visit http://goo.gl/KbBg8M.

All the Action Sequence files have the .xaction extension and should be located in the [BISERVER]/pentaho-solutions folder. This folder also stores system configuration and Pentaho solution files. Pentaho solution is a file generated by the Pentaho design tools, such as Pentaho Reporting, Pentaho Schema Workbench, Pentaho Data Integration.

Action Sequence files can be created using **Pentaho Design Studio**, a desktop client tool. For more information about this tool, visit http://goo.gl/a62gFV.

The JPivot component example

JPivot is an interactive reporting component. It is used to render an **OLAP** (**Online Analytical Processing**) table and to interactively and dynamically explore and navigate data on the table.

You can explore JPivot in PUC as shown in the following steps:

1. In the `BI Developer Examples` solution folder, select `Analysis`, and double-click on the **Quadrant Slice and Dice** menu to open `JPivot` in our working space. You will have a display that looks like the one shown in the following screenshot:

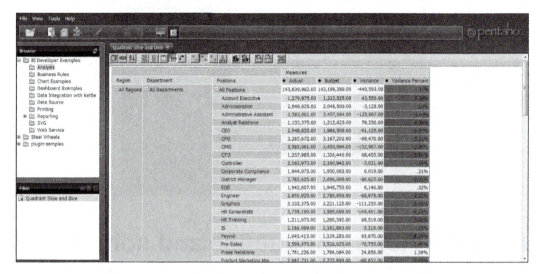

The preceding screenshot shows a tabular pivot view of data variance between budget and actual. If the variance is negative then it will have a red color indicator, otherwise it will have a green one.

2. Right-click on the **Quadrant Slice and Dice** menu to make a contextual menu pop up. Click on **Properties**. Notice that the solution refers to the `query1.xaction` file, which is an Action Sequence file that contains a JPivot display component. The following screenshot shows the properties dialog:

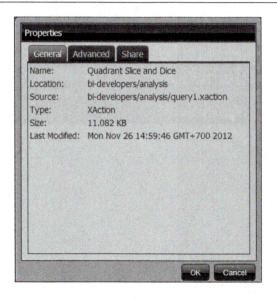

For more information about JPivot, visit `http://jpivot.sourceforge.net`.

The message template component example

Message templates are another component of Action Sequence that can be used to read files such as XML and HTML and combine them with the content generated by other components.

Let's take a look at an example showing an animated SVG from an HTML file:

1. Extract the contents of the `21590S_chapter2.zip` file into `[BISERVER]/pentaho-solutions`.

2. Log in to PUC.

3. In the **Tools** menu, select **Refresh**, and click on **Repository Cache**. The **Chapter 2** menu will show up in the **Browse** pane.

4. In the **Chapter 2** menu, double-click on **Animated Star**.

A page with an animated star image appears. It will look like the one in the following screenshot:

The embedded HSQLDB database server

Pentaho BI Server comes with the **HSQLDB (HyperSQL DataBase)** embedded database server. This application is an open source database server that runs on the Java platform. With HSQLDB we don't need a separate database server to get the web application up and running.

The three databases that come with CE are **hibernate**, **quartz**, and **sampledata**. They are used for storing Pentaho's server configuration, user security and authorization, job schedules, and data samples used by report samples.

The database's physical file is located in [BISERVER]/data. Here you can find the .script, .lck, .properties, and .log files associated with each database. The file with the .script extension is the datafile, .lck is the locking file, .log is the user activities audit file, and .properties is the configuration for the database.

Let's try to explore what's inside the database using a database manager tool that comes with HSQLDB. Start your console application, and execute the following command:

```
java -cp [BISERVER]\data\lib\hsqldb-1.8.0.jar
org.hsqldb.util.DatabaseManagerSwing
```

After a while you'll be asked to fill in the connection details to the database. Use the connection details as shown in the following screenshot, and click on the **OK** button to connect to the hibernate database. The following screenshot shows the connection settings:

The **Database Manager** layout consists of a menu toolbar, a menu bar, and three panels: **Object Browser Pane**, **SQL Query Pane**, and **Result Pane**, as shown in the following screenshot:

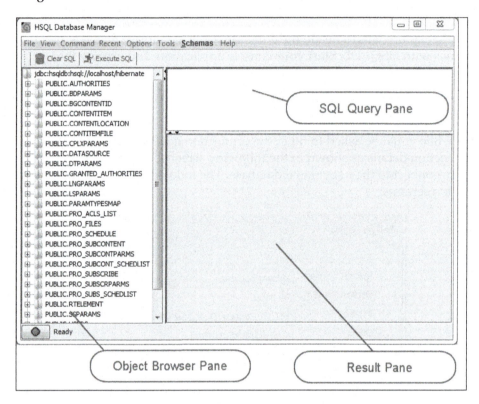

In the query pane, type a SQL command to query a table, followed by *Ctrl* + *E*:

```
Select * from users;
```

We will get a list of data that are part of the PUC users.

The following screenshot shows the default Pentaho users listed in the **Result Pane**:

USERNAME	PASSWORD	DESCRIPTION	ENABLED
admin	c2VjcmV0	[null]	☑
joe	cGFzc3dvcmQ=	[null]	☑
pat	cGFzc3dvcmQ=	[null]	☑
suzy	cGFzc3dvcmQ=	[null]	☑
tiffany	cGFzc3dvcmQ=	[null]	☑

Try to explore other tables from the Object Browser pane, and query the content in the SQL Query pane. You will soon find out that all PUC settings and session activities are stored in this database.

The other databases include **quartz**, which stores data that is related to job scheduling, and **sampledata** that provides data to all the PUC reporting and data-processing examples distributed with the BI Server.

Pentaho Marketplace

Pentaho BI Server CE has several interesting plugins to extend its functionality, but installing and configuring it has proved to be a challenging administration task. It has to be done manually with no friendly user interface available.

To overcome this problem, starting from Version 4.8, Pentaho introduced **Pentaho Marketplace**, a collection of online Pentaho plugins where administrators can browse directly from PUC and set it up using a guided, step-by-step process. In the next example, we will show you how to install **Saiku** — a very popular plugin that provides highly interactive OLAP reporting. For more information about Saiku, visit `http://meteorite.bi/saiku`.

Saiku installation

The following steps describe the installation of Saiku from Pentaho Marketplace:

1. In the PUC **Tools** menu, select **Marketplace**. Alternatively, you can click on the **Pentaho Marketplace** menu bar. The following screenshot shows Pentaho Marketplace:

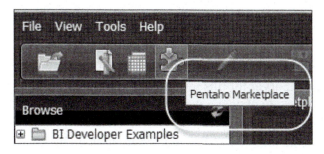

2. A list of plugins that are available in the current version of the BI Server will show up. Plugins that haven't been installed have the option **Install**, and the ones that have newer versions will have the **Upgrade** option. The following screenshot shows the plugin list:

3. Choose **Saiku Analytics**, and click on **Install**. The following screenshot shows the Saiku plugin:

4. The **Do you want to install now?** dialog box will appear. Click on the **OK** button to start the installation process.

5. Wait until the **Successfully Installed** dialog appears.

6. Restart the BI Server for this installation to take effect. Go to the [BISERVER] folder and execute `stop-pentaho.bat` (Windows) or `stop-pentaho.sh` (UNIX/Linux).

7. After all the dialogs close, start the BI Server again by executing `start-`[BISERVER]`/pentaho.bat` (Windows) or [BISERVER]`/start-pentaho.sh` (UNIX/Linux).

8. Re-login to your PUC. The new **Saiku** icon is added to the menu bar. The following screenshot shows the **New Saiku Analytics** icon in the menu bar:

9. Click on the icon to show the **Saiku Analytics** interface. Try to explore the tool. Select an item from the **Cubes** list, and drag an item from **Dimensions** and **Measures** to the workspace. The following screenshot shows a sample Saiku session:

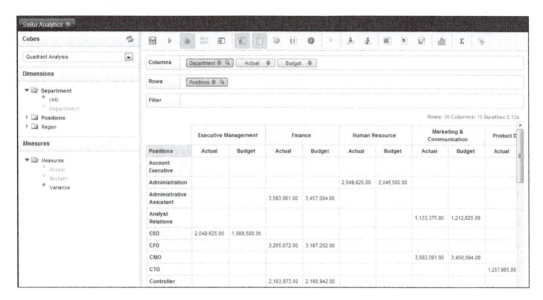

For more information on how to use the application in detail, visit
`http://docs.analytical-labs.com/`.

Pentaho Administration Console (PAC)

Several administration tasks can be done via PUC, but some tasks, such as adding users, adding and assigning roles, and changing passwords, can only be done through PAC.

Running PAC is quite straightforward; execute the startup script `[PAC]/start-pac.bat` (Windows) or `[PAC]/start-pac.sh` (Unix/Linux). In a moment, the console will show that the server has already started.

As it is also a web application, you can access PAC through your web browser. The standard URL and port for PAC is `http://localhost:8099`. The default username/password are `admin/password`, which can be changed. Besides, users/roles can be managed from the PAC console. The following screenshot shows the Pentaho Administration Console (PAC):

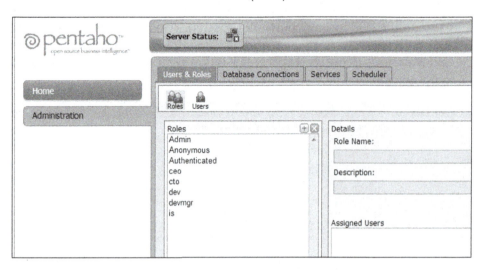

Creating data connections

To finish the chapter, we will show you how to create a MySQL data connection both in PAC and PUC. Follow these steps to create a new data connection from PAC:

1. Click on the **Administration** tab in the left-hand pane.
2. Click on the **Database Connections** tab in the center pane. You will see that there is already one connection defined, **SampleData**. The following screenshot shows the **Database Connections** tab:

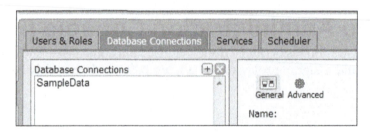

3. Click the plus (**+**) button in the title pane to add a new connection.

4. Fill in the database connection details. The following configurations are taken from my local setup:

   ° **Name**: PHIMinimart

   ° **Driver Class**: com.mysql.jdbc.Driver

   ° **User Name**: root

   ° **Password**: (none)

   ° **URL**: jdbc:mysql://localhost/phi_minimart

   If you are familiar with Java programming, this configuration is actually the JDBC connection string.

5. Click on the **Test** button. If everything is ok, a successful notification dialog appears.

6. Click on the **OK** button to finish the process.

7. The PHIMinimart connection is now available as your data source. The following screenshot shows the new, defined database connection:

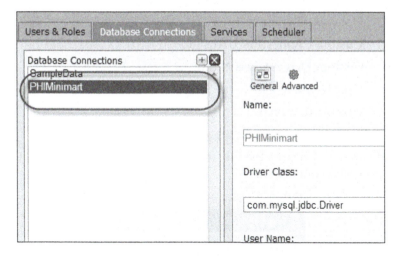

For the following activities, you will need to copy the MySQL JDBC library driver from PAC to BI Server. The library is not included in BI Server distribution by default.

In version 4.8, the JDBC filename is mysql-connector-java-5.1.17.jar. Copy the file from PAC/jdbc, navigate to the BISERVER/tomcat/lib folder and paste the file there. Restart the BI Server once you have copied the file.

Follow these steps for creating a new data connection from PUC:

1. In the **File** menu, click on **New** and select **Data Source...**.

2. If the **Data Source Wizard** appears, fill in the following configuration:
   - **Data Source Name**: PHIDataSource
   - **Source Type**: Database table(s)

3. In the connection setting, click on the green plus (**+**) icon to create a new data connection. The following screenshot shows **Add New Connection** from PUC:

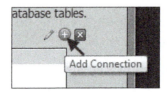

4. If the **Database Connection** dialog appears, type in the following configuration values:
   - **Connection Name**: PHIMinimart2
   - **Database Type**: Generic Database
   - **Custom Connection URL**: jdbc:mysql://localhost/phi_minimart
   - **Custom Driver Class Name**: com.mysql.jdbc.Driver
   - **User Name**: root
   - **Password**: (none)

5. Click on the **Test** button. If everything is ok, the dialog showing success should appear. Click on the **OK** button. The following screenshot shows the successful connection:

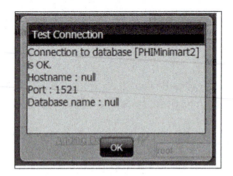

6. Click on the **OK** button.

7. Now you have a new, defined connection. The following screenshot shows a new connection in PUC.

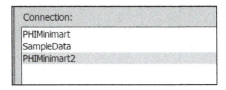

8. For the sole purpose of creating a connection, I'll not continue to the next step in the wizard. Click on the **Cancel** button.

9. If you want to make sure the connection already exists, you can recheck the connection list in PAC. The following screenshot shows the connection list in PAC:

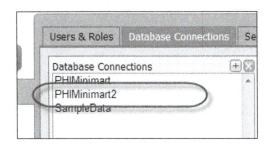

Now, we have successfully set up both connections to a MySQL database. We will learn how to use a data connection with several sources later in this book.

Summary

Pentaho BI Server is a Community Edition (CE) equivalent to BA Server of the Enterprise Edition (EE). They have differences in regards to core applications and configuration tools. Although this book focuses on CE, all the samples actually work with EE if you decide to switch. The BI Server comprises of two web applications, which are Pentaho User Console (PUC) and Pentaho Administration Console (PAC).

Throughout this chapter, we showed you how to obtain, install, run, and use the BI Server, PUC, and PAC.

This chapter also briefly explained what Pentaho solution and Pentaho Action Sequence files are. They will serve as the building blocks of Pentaho content and process development.

Pentaho Marketplace is a new, exciting feature that makes it easy for administrators to add new features easily from PUC. Through an example walkthrough process, we installed Saiku—a popular Pentaho plugin—using this feature.

Finally, we also learned how to administer data connections using both PUC and PAC.

With all of this set up, we are good to go to the next chapter, *Churning Big Data with Pentaho*.

3
Churning Big Data with Pentaho

This chapter provides a basic understanding of the Big Data ecosystem and an example to analyze data sitting on the Hadoop framework using Pentaho. At the end of this chapter, you will learn how to translate diverse data sets into meaningful data sets using Hadoop/Hive.

In this chapter we will cover the following topics:

- Overview of Big Data and Hadoop
- Hadoop architecture
- Big Data capabilities of Pentaho Data Integration (PDI)
- Working with PDI and Hortonworks Data Platform, a Hadoop distribution
- Loading data from HDFS to Hive using PDI
- Query data using Hive's SQL-like language

An overview of Big Data and Hadoop

Today, Big Data (`http://en.wikipedia.org/wiki/Big_data`) and Hadoop (`http://hadoop.apache.org`) have almost become synonyms of each other. Theoretically, the former is a notion whereas the latter is a software platform.

Big Data

Whenever we think of massive amounts of data, Google immediately pops up in our head. In fact, **Big Data** was first recognized in its true sense by Google in 2004, and a white paper was written on **Google File System** (**GFS**) and MapReduce; two years later, Hadoop was born. Similarly, after Google published the open source projects Sawzall and BigTable, Pig, Hive, and HBase were born. Even in the future, Google is going to drive this story forward.

Big Data is a combination of data management technologies that have evolved over a period of time. Big Data is a term used to define a large collection of data (or data sets) that can be structured, unstructured, or mixed, and quickly grows so large that it becomes difficult to manage using conventional databases or statistical tools. Another way to define this term is any data source that has at least three of the following shared characteristics (known as 3Vs):

- Extremely large *volume* of data
- Extremely high *velocity* of data
- Extremely wide *variety* of data

Sometimes, two more Vs are added for *variability* and *value*. Some interesting statistics of data explosion are as follows:

- There are 2 billion Internet users in the world
- 6.8 billion mobile phones by the end of 2012 (more people have cellphones than toilets!)
- 8 TB of data is processed by Twitter every day (this translates to 100 MB per second; our normal hard disk writes with the speed of 80 MB per second)
- Facebook processes more than 500 TB of data every day!
- 90 percent of the world's data has been generated over the last two years

Interestingly, 80 percent of Big Data is unstructured, and businesses now need fast, reliable, and deeper data insight.

Hadoop

Hadoop, an open source project from Apache Software Foundation, has become the de facto standard for storing, processing, and analyzing hundreds of terabytes, even petabytes of data. This framework was originally developed by Doug Cutting and Mike Cafarella in 2005, and named it after Doug's son's toy elephant. Written in Java, this framework is optimized to handle massive amounts of structured/unstructured data through parallelism using MapReduce on GoogleFS with the help of inexpensive commodity hardware.

> Hadoop is used for Big Data complements, OLTP and OLAP. It is certainly not a replacement to a relational database.

Hadoop is a highly *scalable* model and supports unlimited linear scalability. It runs on commodity hardware, which is $1/10^{th}$ of the enterprise hardware, and uses open source software. So, it can run 10 times faster at the same cost. It is *distributed* and *reliable*: by default, it keeps three times data redundancy, which can be further configured.

Hadoop, over a period of time, has become a full-fledged ecosystem by adding lots of new open source friends such as Hive, Pig, HBase, and ZooKeeper.

There are many Internet or social networking companies such as Yahoo!, Facebook, Amazon, eBay, Twitter, and LinkedIn that use Hadoop. Yahoo! Search Webmap was the largest Hadoop application when it went into production in 2008, with more than 10,000 core Linux clusters. As of today, Yahoo! has more than 40,000 nodes running in more than 20 Hadoop clusters.

Facebook's Hadoop clusters include the largest single **HDFS (Hadoop Distributed File System)** cluster known, with more than 100 PB physical disk space in a single HDFS filesystem.

The Hadoop architecture

Hadoop is a large scale, large-batch data processing system, which uses MapReduce for computation and HDFS for data storage. HDFS is the most reliable distributed filesystem with a configurable replication mechanism designed to be deployed on low-cost commodity hardware.

HDFS breaks files into chunks of a minimum of 64 MB blocks, where each block is replicated three times. The replication factor can be configured, and it has to be perfectly balanced depending upon the data. The following diagram depicts a typical two node Hadoop cluster set up on two bare metal machines, although you can use a virtual machine as well.

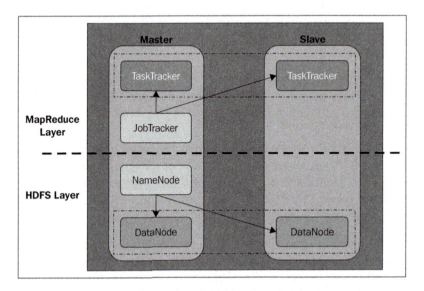

One of these is the master node, and the other one is the worker/slave node. The master node consists of JobTracker and NameNode. In the preceding diagram, the master node also acts as the slave as there are only two nodes in the illustration. There can be multiple slave nodes, but we have taken a single node for illustration purposes. A slave node, also known as a worker node, can act as a data node as well as a task tracker, though one can configure to have data-only worker nodes for data-intensive operations and compute-only worker nodes for CPU-intensive operations. Starting this Hadoop cluster can be performed in two steps: by starting HDFS daemons (NameNode and data node) and then starting MapReduce daemons (JobTracker and TaskTracker).

In a big cluster, there are dedicated roles to nodes; for example, HDFS is managed by a dedicated server to host the filesystem containing the `edits` logfile, which will be merged with `fsimage` at the startup time of NameNode. A secondary NameNode (SNN) keeps merging `fsimage` with `edits` regularly with configurable intervals (checkpoint or snapshot). The primary NameNode is a single point of failure for the cluster, and SNN reduces the risk by minimizing the downtime and loss of data.

Similarly, a standalone JobTracker server manages job scheduling whenever the job is submitted to the cluster. It is also a single point of failure. It will monitor all the TaskTracker nodes and, in case one task fails, it will relaunch that task automatically, possibly on a different TaskTracker node.

For the effective scheduling of tasks, every Hadoop supported filesystem should provide location consciousness, meaning that it should have the name of the rack (more incisively, of the network switch) where a worker node is. Hadoop applications can use this information while executing work on the respective node. HDFS uses this approach to create data replication efficiently by keeping data on different racks so that even when one rack goes down, data will still be served by the other rack.

The filesystem is at the bottom and the MapReduce engine is stacked above it. The MapReduce engine consists of a single JobTracker, which can be related to an order taker. Clients submit their MapReduce job requests to JobTracker that in turn passes the requests to the available TaskTracker from the cluster, with the intention of keeping the work as close to the data as possible. If work cannot be started on the worker node where the data is residing, then priority is assigned in the same rack with the intention of reducing the network traffic. If a TaskTracker server fails or times out for some reason, that part of the job will be rescheduled. The TaskTracker server is always a lightweight process to ensure reliability, and it's achieved by spawning off new processes when new jobs come to be processed on the respective node. The TaskTracker sends heartbeats periodically to the JobTracker to update the status. The JobTracker's and TaskTracker's current status and information can be viewed from a web browser.

At the time of writing, Hadoop 2 was still in alpha, but it would be worthwhile to mention its significant new enhancements here. Hadoop 2 has three major enhancements, namely, HDFS failover, Federated Namenode, and MapReduce 2.0 (MRv2) or YARN. There are a few distributions such as CDH4 (Cloudera's Distribution of Hadoop) and HDP2 (Hortonworks Data Platform), which are bundling Hadoop 2.0. Everywhere else, Hadoop is referred to as Hadoop 1.

The Hadoop ecosystem

Hadoop, along with its community friends, makes a complete ecosystem. This ecosystem is continuously evolving with a large number of open source contributors. The following diagram gives a high-level overview of the Hadoop ecosystem:

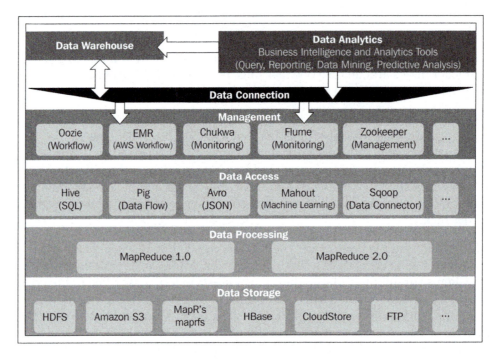

The Hadoop ecosystem is logically divided into five layers that are self-explanatory. Some of the ecosystem components are explained as follows:

- **Data Storage**: This is where the raw data resides. There are multiple filesystems supported by Hadoop, and there are also connectors available for the data warehouse (DW) and relational databases as shown:
    - **HDFS**: This is a distributed filesystem that comes with the Hadoop framework. It uses the TCP/IP layer for communication. An advantage of using HDFS is its data intelligence as that determines what data resides within which worker node.
    - **Amazon S3**: This is a filesystem from Amazon Web Services (AWS), which is an Internet-based storage. As it is fully controlled by AWS in their cloud, data intelligence is not possible with the Hadoop master and efficiency could be lower because of network traffic.

- ° **MapR-FS**: This provides higher availability, transactionally correct snapshots, and higher performance than HDFS. MapR-FS comes with MapR's Hadoop distribution.

- ° **HBase**: This is a columnar, multidimensional database derived from Google's BigTable. Based on the HDFS filesystem, it maintains data in partitions and, therefore, can give data access efficiently in a sorted manner.

- **Data Access**: This layer helps in accessing the data from various data stores, shown as follows:

  - ° **Hive**: This is a data warehouse infrastructure with SQL-like querying capabilities on Hadoop data sets. Its power lies in the SQL interface that helps to quickly check/validate the data, which makes it quite popular in the developer community.

  - ° **Pig**: This is a data flow engine and multiprocess execution framework. Its scripting language is called **Pig Latin**. The Pig interpreter translates these scripts into MapReduce jobs, so even if you are a business user, you can execute the scripts and study the data analysis in the Hadoop cluster.

  - ° **Avro**: This is one of the data serialization systems, which provides a rich data format, a container file to store persistent data, a remote procedure call, and so on. It uses JSON to define data types, and data is serialized in compact binary data.

  - ° **Mahout**: This is a machine learning software with core algorithms as (use- and item-based) recommendation or batch-based collaborative filtering, classification, and clustering. The core algorithms are implemented on top of Apache Hadoop using the MapReduce paradigm, though it can also be used outside the Hadoop world as a math library focused on linear algebra and statistics.

  - ° **Sqoop**: This is designed to scoop up bulk data expeditiously between Apache Hadoop and structured data stores such as relational databases. Sqoop has become a top-level Apache project since March 2012. You could also call it an ETL tool for Hadoop. It uses the MapReduce algorithm to import or export data supporting parallel processing as well as fault tolerance.

- **Management layer**: This comprises of tools that assist in administering the Hadoop infrastructure and are shown as follows:

    ◦ **Oozie**: This is a workflow scheduler system to manage Apache Hadoop jobs. It is a server-based workflow engine, where workflow is a collection of actions such as Hadoop MapReduce, Pig/Hive/Sqoop jobs arranged in a control dependency DAG (Directed Acyclic Graph). Oozie is a scalable, reliable, and extensible system.

    ◦ **Elastic MapReduce (EMR)**: This provisions the Hadoop cluster, running and terminating jobs, and also handling data transfers between EC2 and S3 are automated by Amazon's Elastic MapReduce.

    ◦ **Chukwa**: This is an open source data collection system for monitoring large, distributed systems. Chukwa is built on top of HDFS and the MapReduce framework, and inherits Hadoop's scalability and robustness. Chukwa also includes a flexible and powerful toolkit for displaying, monitoring, and analyzing results to make the best use of the collected data.

    ◦ **Flume**: This is a distributed service comprising of multiple agents, which essentially sit outside the Hadoop cluster, to collect and aggregate streaming data (for example, log data) efficiently. It has a fault tolerant mechanism, using which it can act as a reliable streaming data feed to HDFS for real-time analysis.

    ◦ **ZooKeeper**: This is another Apache Software Foundation project, which provides open source distributed coordination and synchronization services as well as a naming registry for large distributed systems. ZooKeeper's architecture supports high availability through redundant services. It uses a hierarchical filesystem and is fault tolerant and high performing, facilitating loose coupling. ZooKeeper is already being used by many Apache projects such as HDFS and HBase, as well as its run in production by Yahoo!, Facebook, and Rackspace.

- **Data Analytics**: This is the area where a lot of third-party vendors provide various proprietary as well as open source tools. A few of them are as follows:

    ◦ **Pentaho**: This has the capability of Data Integration (Kettle), analytics, reporting, creating dashboards, and predictive analytics directly from the Hadoop nodes. It is available with enterprise support as well as the community edition.

    ◦ **Storm**: This is a free and open source distributed, fault tolerant, and real-time computation system for unbounded streams of data.

° **Splunk**: This is an enterprise application, which can perform real-time and historical searches, reporting, and statistical analysis. It also provides the cloud-based flavor, Splunk Storm.

 The real advantages of Hadoop are its scalability, reliability, open source software, distributed data, more data better than complex algorithms, and schema on read. It has non-batch components like HBase.

While setting up the Hadoop ecosystem, you can either do the setup on your own or use third-party distributions from vendors such as Amazon, MapR, Cloudera, Hortonworks, and others. Third-party distributions may cost you a little extra, but it takes away the complexity of maintaining and supporting the system and you can focus on the business problem.

Hortonworks Sandbox

For the purpose of learning the basics of Pentaho and its Big Data features, we will use a Hortonworks Hadoop distribution virtual machine. Hortonworks Sandbox is a single-node implementation of the enterprise-ready **Hortonworks Data Platform** (**HDP**). HDP combines the most useful and stable version of Apache Hadoop and its related projects into a single tested and certified package. Included in this implementation are some good tutorials and easy-to-use tools accessible via a web browser.

We will use this VM as our working Hadoop framework throughout the book. When you're proficient with the use of this tool, you can apply your skills for a large-scale Hadoop cluster.

See *Appendix A, Big Data Sets*, for the complete installation, configuration, and sample data preparation guide.

Pentaho Data Integration (PDI)

In the previous chapter, we discussed **Pentaho Data Integration** (PDI) a little, which is a part of the Pentaho stack. The Pentaho ecosystem enables management of voluminous data with ease and also provides increased velocity and variety. (It does not matter how many data sources or whichever data types…!) PDI delivers "analytics ready" data to end users much faster with a choice of visual tools that reduce the time and complexity of the data analytics life cycle. PDI comes as a standalone Community Edition (CE) as well as bundled with Pentaho BA Server Enterprise Edition (EE).

PDI has some inherent advantages such as beautiful orchestration and integration for all data stores using its very powerful GUI. It has an adaptive Big Data Layer supporting almost any Big Data source with reduced complexity. In this way, data has become abstract from analytics giving a competitive advantage. Its simple drag-and-drop design supports a rich set of mapping objects, including a GUI-based MapReduce designer for Hadoop, with support for custom plugins developed in Java.

Just a month back, Rackspace brought ETL to the Cloud with help from Pentaho, so you don't need to jam your local hardware but you would rather leverage this online service.

Now we will explore much of the capabilities throughout the remainder of the chapter. The latest stable version of PDI at the time of this writing was 4.4. You can obtain the distribution from SourceForge at `http://goo.gl/95Ikgp`.

Download `pdi-ce-4.4.0-stable.zip` or `4.4.0-stable.tar.gz`. Extract it to any location you prefer. We will refer to the extraction's full path as `[PDI_HOME]`.

For running PDI for the first time, follow these steps:

1. Navigate to `[PDI_HOME]` and double-click on `Spoon.bat`. This will launch Spoon, a GUI application to design and execute a PDI script (job or transformation).

2. The **Repository Connection** dialog appears; uncheck the **Show this dialog at startup** option and click on the **Cancel** button to close it.

3. The **Spoon Tips...** dialog appears; click on **Close**.

4. The **Spoon** application window appears to create a job and transformation.

The Pentaho Big Data plugin configuration

PDI 4.4 comes with a Big Data plugin that is not compatible with Hortonworks distribution. We need to download and configure PDI with the new version of the plugin to make it work. Close any Spoon application if you are running it.

To set up the Big Data plugin for PDI, follow these given steps:

1. Visit `http://ci.pentaho.com`.

2. Click on the **Big Data** menu tab.

3. Click on `pentaho-big-data-plugin-1.3` or the latest project available.

4. Download the ZIP version of the `pentaho-big-data-plugin` file. At the time of this writing, the latest version of the file was `pentaho-big-data-plugin-1.3-SNAPSHOT.zip`.

The following screenshot shows the latest version of the Pentaho Big Data plugin:

5. Delete the `[PDI_HOME]/plugins/pentaho-big-data-plugin` folder. Replace it with the contents of the ZIP file.

6. Edit the `[PDI_HOME]/plugins/pentaho-big-data-plugin/plugin.properties` file and change the `active.hadoop.configuration` property from `hadoop-20` to `hdp12`, which represents the Hadoop Data Platform.

7. Copy the `core-site.xml` file from VM's `/etc/hadoop/conf.empty` folder using a secure FTP (see *Appendix B, Hadoop Setup*) into `[PDI_HOME]/plugins/pentaho-big-data-plugin/hadoop-configurations/hdp12/`. Edit the file by replacing the sandbox host to a working IP address.

8. Extract the `[PDI_HOME]/plugins/pentaho-big-data-plugin/pentaho-mapreduce-libraries.zip` file into any folder you prefer. We will refer to the extraction full path as `[PDI_MR_LIB]`.

9. Delete `[PDI_HOME]/libext/JDBC/pentaho-hadoop-hive-jdbc-shim-1.3.0.jar` and replace it with `[PDI_MR_LIB]/lib/pentaho-hadoop-hive-jdbc-shim-1.3-SNAPSHOT.jar`.

10. Copy the `[PDI_MR_LIB]/lib/pentaho-hadoop-shims-api-1.3-SNAPSHOT.jar` file into the `[PDI_HOME]/libext/` folder.

11. Delete `[PDI_HOME]/lib/kettle-core.jar` and replace the file with `[PDI_MR_LIB]/lib/kettle-core-4.4.2-SNAPSHOT.jar`.

12. Delete `[PDI_HOME]/lib/kettle-db.jar` and replace the file with `[PDI_MR_LIB]/lib/kettle-db-4.4.2-SNAPSHOT.jar`.

13. Delete `[PDI_HOME]/lib/kettle-engine.jar` and replace the file with `[PDI_MR_LIB]/lib/kettle-engine-4.4.2-SNAPSHOT.jar`.

14. Copy and replace all the following remaining jars from `[PDI_MR_LIB]/lib` into `[PDI_HOME]/libext`.

Importing data to Hive

Before we begin the walkthrough, see *Appendix A, Big Data Sets*, to complete the Hive nyse_stocks data preparation and follow these steps:

1. Launch Spoon if you have closed it.
2. On the **File** menu, click on **New** and select **Transformation**.
3. On the left-hand side panel, click on the **View** tab.
4. Right-click on the **Database connections** node to show up a contextual menu and choose **New**.

The following screenshot shows you how to create a new database connection:

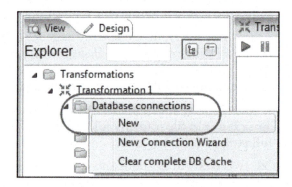

When the **Database Connection** dialog appears, fill in the following configuration:

- **Connection Name**: HIVE2
- **Connection Type**: Hadoop Hive 2
- **Host Name**: [your working IP address]
- **Database Name**: default

Now follow these steps:

1. Click on the **Test** button to verify the connection. If successful, click on the **OK** button to close it. The display window will look like the following screenshot:

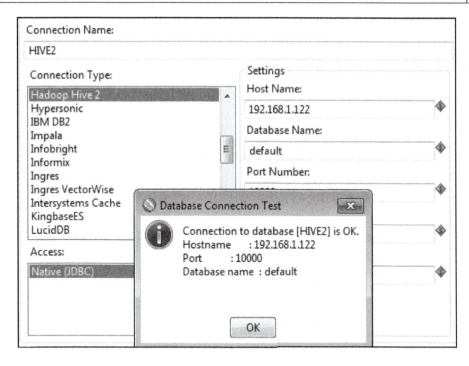

2. On the left-hand side panel, click on the **Design** tab.

3. In the **Input** group, click on the **Table input** step and drag it into the working space. The following screenshot shows how the **Table input** step can be put into the working space:

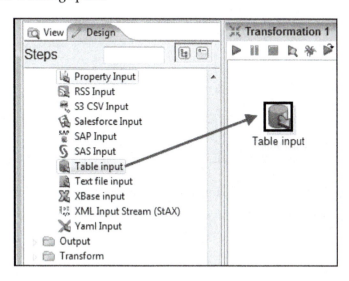

4. Double-click on the **Table input** step and the editor appears. On the connection listbox, select **HIVE2**. Type the following query into the SQL editor pane. Set the **Limit Size** parameter to 65535. We plan to export the data to an Excel file; the 65535 threshold is the limit up to which an Excel file is able to store data.

```
SELECT * FROM nyse_stocks
```

5. Click on the **Preview** button; the preview dialog appears, and then click on the **OK** button. Shortly, it will show a data preview of nyse_stocks, a Hive table.

This process is actually a Hadoop MapReduce job; see the *Preparing Hive data* section in *Appendix B, Hadoop Setup*, which shows the job logs.

The following screenshot shows a data preview of the Hive query:

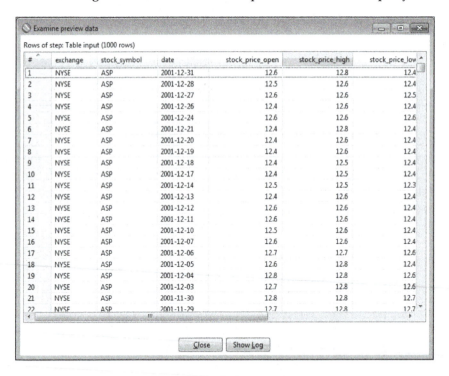

6. Click on the **Close** and **OK** buttons, respectively, to close all the open dialogs.

7. On the **File** menu, choose **Save** and name the file export-hive-to-excel.ktr.

8. In the **Output** group, choose and put the **Microsoft Excel Output** step into the workspace. The following screenshot shows the newly added **Microsoft Excel Output** step:

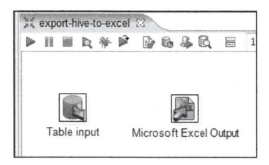

9. Press *Ctrl* + click on the **Table input** step followed by pressing *Ctrl* + click on the **Microsoft Excel Output** step. Right-click on one of the steps—a contextual dialog will pop up—and choose **New Hop**. A hop represents data or control flow among steps. Make sure the configuration looks similar to the following screenshot; click on the **OK** button.

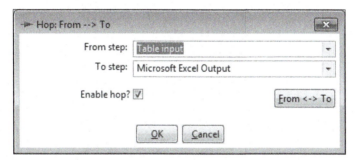

Your transformation will look similar to the following screenshot:

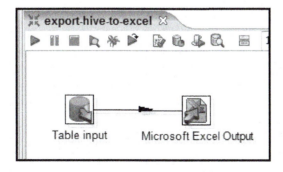

10. Double-click on **Microsoft Excel Output**; the editor dialog appears. On the
    File tab, specify your output filename in the **Filename** textbox. Click on the
    OK button to close the dialog. The following screenshot shows a **Microsoft
    Excel Output** step dialog:

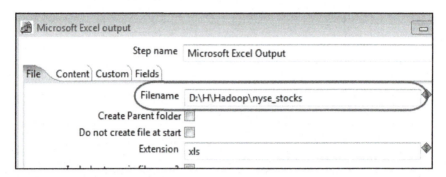

11. On the menu bar, right below the transformation tab, click on the **Run
    this transformation or job** button. On the **Execute a transformation** dialog,
    click on the **Launch** button. The following screenshot shows the running of a
    transformation or job menu in PDI:

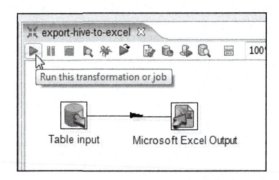

12. If the transformation runs successfully, explore the data transfer activity metrics. The following screenshot shows that the transformation runs in 58 seconds:

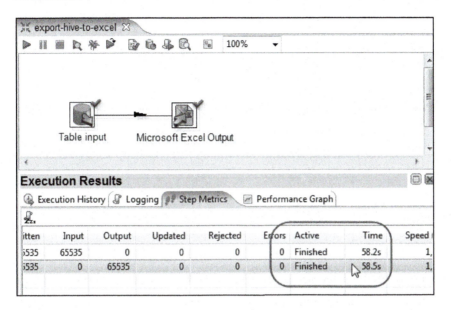

13. Open the Excel file result. The displayed data will look similar to the following screenshot:

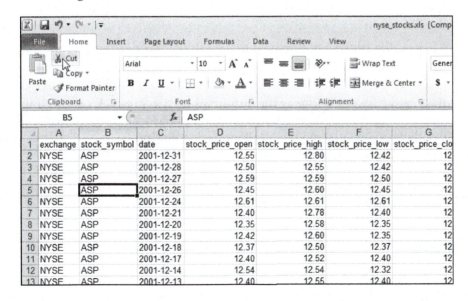

Putting a data file into HDFS

The previous example shows how PDI interacts with Hive using a SQL-like expression.

Now let's work with the framework filesystem, HDFS. We will copy a CSV text file into an HDFS folder. Follow these steps:

1. Download a compressed CSV sample file from `http://goo.gl/EdJwk5`.

2. Create a new job from Spoon.

3. Put data in the workspace and create a flow between the following steps:

    ○ From the **General** grouping, choose **START**

    ○ From the **Big Data** grouping, choose **Hadoop Copy Files**

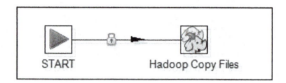

4. Double-click on **Hadoop Copy Files**. The step's editor dialog will appear.

5. Click on the **Browse** button next to the **File/Folder** textbox. The **Open File** dialog appears; choose the file you have downloaded from step 1 and click on **OK** to close the dialog.

6. Remove the `gz:` prefix and exclamation mark symbol (`!`) suffix from the filename.

7. Click on the **Browse** button next to the **File/Folder destination** textbox.

8. Type in your HDFS server IP address and click on the **Connect** button. It may take a while before a connection is established. Once connected, select the `/user/sample` folder as the output folder. Do not click on **OK** at this stage, but rather copy the URL on to the clipboard. Click on **Cancel**. Paste the clipboard result into the **File/Folder destination** field.

9. Click on the **Add** button to put the filename path into the grid.

10. Save the job's filename as `hdfs_copy.kjb`.

11. Run the job.

The following screenshot shows the HDFS file browser dialog:

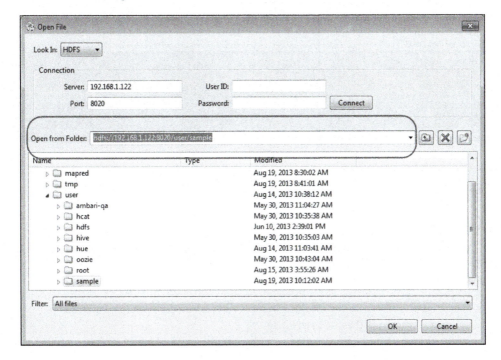

The following screenshot shows the local and remote HDFS paths:

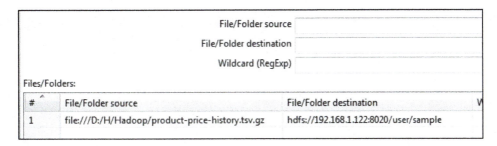

12. Once the job is finished, you can validate whether the file has been successfully copied into HDFS or not by issuing the following command:

```
hadoop fs  -ls /user/sample/
```

The following screenshot shows the HDFS content after the copy process:

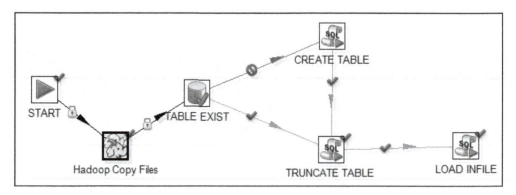

Loading data from HDFS into Hive (job orchestration)

Now we have a text file residing in HDFS that can further be processed using the MapReduce job. Behind all the SQL is a MapReduce job. We will use the Pentaho Data Integration SQL-related step to demonstrate this capability. Follow these steps:

1. Launch Spoon if it is not running.

2. Open `hdfs_to_hive_product_price_history.kjb` from the chapter's code bundle folder. Load the file into Spoon. You should see a job flow similar to the one shown in the following screenshot:

3. The **Hadoop Copy Files** step is responsible for copying the `product-price-history.tsv.gz` file from the local folder into HDFS.

4. The **TABLE EXIST** step checks whether the `product_price_history` table exists in Hive or not. If it does not, it continues to the **CREATE TABLE** or **TRUNCATE TABLE** step. The step editor dialog looks like the one shown in the following screenshot:

5. The **CREATE TABLE** step executes the SQL command to create a new `product_price_history` table with its structure. The editor looks like the one shown in the following screenshot:

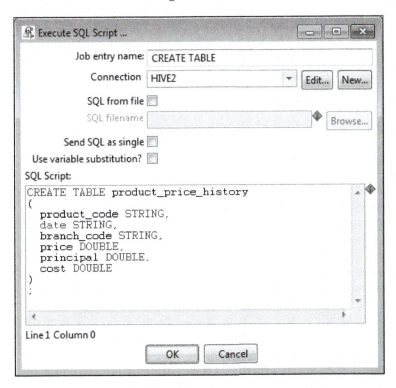

Hive does not support the DATE data type, so we use STRING instead, in this case, for the date field.

6. The **TRUNCATE TABLE** step is executed if the table exists. This step will remove all data from the table.

7. Finally, the **LOAD INFILE** step will load the content of the uploaded file into the product_price_history table. It reads from a HDFS location. The step editor dialog looks like the one shown in the following screenshot:

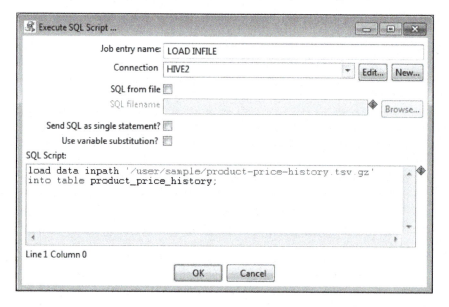

8. Run the job.

9. Launch your browser and navigate to Hortonworks Sandbox as shown in the following screenshot:

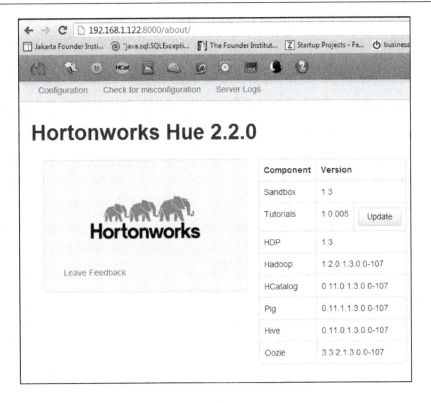

10. From the menu bar, choose **Beeswax (Hive UI)**, as shown in the following screenshot:

11. Click on the **Tables** menu.

12. From the list of table names, make sure `product_price_history` exists. Click on the table.

13. The **Table metadata** page appears; click on the **Columns** tab to show the metadata. Click on the **Samples** tab to see a preview of the data that has already been uploaded using the PDI job.

Using the same process, the `hdfs_to_hive_product_nyse_stocks.kjb` sample file will load a bigger `NYSE-2000-2001.tsv.gz` file data into Hive. At this point, you should have a straightforward understanding of the job.

Summary

This chapter begins with an introduction to the concept of Hadoop, which provides us with a deeper understanding of its distributed architecture on storages and processes, why and when we will use it, its working mechanism, and how the distributed job/task tracker works.

Following the introduction is the walkthrough of Pentaho Data Integration working on Hortonworks Sandbox, one of the Hadoop distributions, that is suitable for learning Hadoop. The chapter shows you how to read and write a datafile to HDFS, import it to Hive, and query the data using a SQL-like language.

In the following chapters, we will discuss how to extend the usage of Hadoop with the help of other Pentaho tools and present it visually using CTools, a community driven visualization tool.

4

Pentaho Business Analytics Tools

This chapter gives a quick overview of the business analytics life cycle. We will look at various tools such as Pentaho Action Sequence and Pentaho Report Designer, as well as the **Community Dashboard Editor (CDE)** and **Community Dashboard Framework (CDF)** plugins and their configuration, and get some hands-on experience of them.

The business analytics life cycle

There could be various steps while performing analytics on Big Data. Generally, there are three stages as depicted in the following diagram:

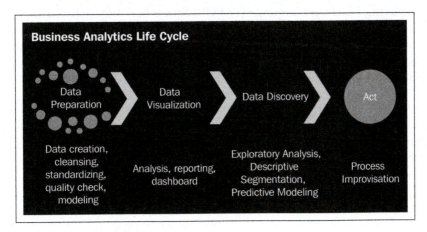

The following list gives a brief description of the three stages depicted in the preceding diagram:

- **Data Preparation**: This stage involves activities from data creation (ETL) to bringing data on to a common platform. In this stage, you will check the quality of the data, cleanse and condition it, and remove unwanted noise. The structure of the data will dictate which tools and analytic techniques can be used. For example, if it contains textual data, sentiment analysis should be used, while if it contains structured financial data, perhaps regression via R analytics platform is the right method. A few more analytical techniques are MapReduce, **Natural language processing** (**NLP**), clustering (k-means clustering), and graph theory (social network analysis).

- **Data Visualization**: This is the next stage after preparation of data. Micro-level analytics will take place here, feeding this data to the reporting engine that supports various visualization plugins. Visualization is a rapidly expanding discipline that not only supports Big Data but can enable enterprises to collaborate more effectively, analyze real-time and historical data for faster trading, develop new models and theories, consolidate IT infrastructure, or demonstrate past, current, and future datacenter performance. This is very handy when you are observing a neatly composed dashboard by a business analyst team.

- **Data Discovery**: This will be the final stage where data miners, statisticians, and data scientists will use enriched data and using visual analysis they can drill into data for greater insight. There are various visualization techniques to find patterns and anomalies, such as geo mapping, heat grids, and scatter/bubble charts. **Predictive analysis** based on the **Predictive Modeling Markup Language** (**PMML**) comes in handy here. Using standard analysis and reporting, data scientists and analysts can uncover meaningful patterns and correlations otherwise hidden. Sophisticated and advanced analytics such as time series forecasting help plan for future outcomes based on a better understanding of prior business performance.

Pentaho gives you a complete end-to-end solution to execute your analytic plan. It helps modeling the data using its rich visual development environment (drag-and-drop supported data integration platform). It is so easy that BI experts and traditional IT developers can offer Big Data to their organization almost effortlessly. It runs natively across the Hadoop clusters for releveraging its distributed data storage and processing capabilities for unmatched scalability.

It analyzes data across multiple dimensions and sources. It has rich visualization and data exploration capabilities that give business users insight into and analysis of their data, which helps in identifying patterns and trends.

 About 2.5 quintillion bytes of data is created every day and the count is doubling every year. Yet only 0.5 percent of that data is being analyzed!

Preparing data

Pentaho Data Integration (PDI) is a great tool to prepare data thanks to its rich data connectors. We will not discuss PDI further here as we already discussed it in the latter part of *Chapter 3, Churning Big Data with Pentaho*.

Preparing BI Server to work with Hive

Before you proceed to the following examples, complete the steps listed in *Appendix B, Hadoop Setup*. Note that all the remaining examples work with the `192.168.1.122` IP address configuration at Hortonworks Sandbox VM.

The following steps will help you prepare BI Server to work with Hive:

1. Copy the `pentaho-hadoop-hive-jdbc-shim-1.3-SNAPSHOT.jar` and `pentaho-hadoop-shims-api-1.3-SNAPSHOT.jar` files into the `[BISERVER]/administration-console/jdbc` and `[BISERVER]/biserver-ce/tomcat/lib` folders respectively. See *Chapter 3, Churning Big Data with Pentaho*, for information on how to obtain the JAR files.

2. Launch **Pentaho User Console (PUC)**.

3. Copy the `Chapter 4` folder from the book's code bundle folder into `[BISERVER]/pentaho-solutions`.

4. From the **Tools** menu, choose **Refresh** and then **Repository Cache**.

5. In the **Browse** pane, you should see a newly added `Chapter 4` folder. Click on the folder.

6. In the **Files** pane, double-click on the **Show Tables in HIVE** menu. If all goes well, the engine will execute an action sequence file — that is, `hive_show_tables.xaction` — and you will see the following screenshot that shows four tables contained in the HIVE database:

The `.xaction` file gets the result — a PDI transformation file — by executing the `hive_show_tables.ktr` file.

 If you want more information about Action Sequence and the client tool to design the `.xaction` file, see `http://goo.gl/6NyxYZ` and `http://goo.gl/WgHbhE`.

Executing and monitoring a Hive MapReduce job

The following steps will guide you to execute and monitor a Hive MapReduce job:

1. While still in the **Files** pane, double-click on the **PDI-Hive Java Query** menu. This will execute `hive_java_query.xaction`, which in turn will execute the `hive_java_query.ktr` PDI transformation. This will take longer to display the result than the previous one.

2. While this is executing, launch a web browser and type in the job's browser address, `http://192.168.1.122:8000/jobbrowser`.

3. Remove **hue** from the **Username** textbox. In the **Job status** listbox, choose **Running**. You will find that there is one job running as an anonymous user. The page will then look like the following screenshot:

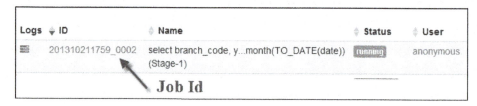

4. Click on the **Job Id** link, the **Recent Tasks** page appears, which lists a MapReduce process stage. Refresh the page until all the steps are complete. The page will look like the following screenshot:

Recent Tasks

Logs ▲ Tasks	⇕ Type
▤ m_000000	MAP
▤ m_000001	JOB_CLEANUP
▤ m_000002	JOB_SETUP
▤ r_000000	REDUCE

5. Back to PUC, you will find the Hive query result, which is actually a MapReduce process result.

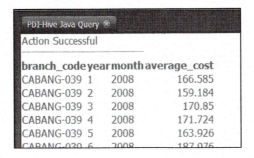

Pentaho Reporting

Pentaho Reporting is a predefined reporting suite with the ability to connect to rich data sources, including PDI transformation. It cannot have a dynamic matrix layout like that of OLAP's pivoting report, but it has the ability to include other rich-user interactivities. **PRD (Pentaho Report Designer)** is a client designer tool to create a Pentaho Reporting report. We will briefly explain the usage of PRD and the report's file format.

The solution file for the report will be in a compressed file format and has the .prpt extension. The reporting engine then parses and renders the file's content into an HTML page or in any other format that we choose. HTML resources such as cascading style sheets, JavaScripts, or image files can be included in the .prpt file. If you have any compression tool such as 7-Zip, try to explore one of the reporting samples distributed with Pentaho BI Server.

For example, the following screenshot shows the files contained in the `[BISERVER]/pentaho-solutions/steel-wheels/reports/Income Statement.prpt` file. Note that inside the `resources` folder, we have two images that serve as the report's logo. The `.xml` files will define the behaviors and items that the report has in place.

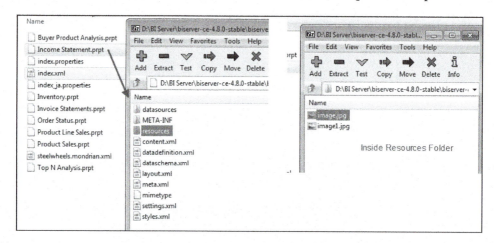

Open this report through PUC. In the **Steel Wheels** folder, select **Reporting** and double-click on **Income Statement**. Note that the report has a list of output formats and **PDF** format is selected by default. Other options listed are **HTML (Single Page)**, **HTML (Paginated)**, **Excel**, **Comma Separated Value**, and so on.

The report also has two images, the logo and background—the same images that we explored in the `Income Statement.prpt` file.

The following screenshot shows the `Income Statement` report sample:

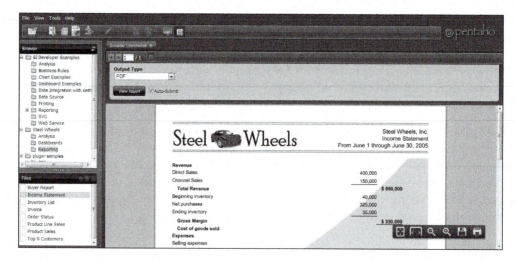

The following steps will help you explore a PRD sample report:

1. Download and extract the PRD distribution from Pentaho's SourceForge project at `http://goo.gl/hxzWdA`. At the time of writing, the latest version is 3.9.1.

2. Run `report-designer.bat`. Close all the dialogs as they are unnecessary now.

3. Click on the **File** menu and choose **Open...**. Then navigate to `[BISERVER]` | `pentaho-solutions` | `steel-wheels` | `reports` | `Income Statement. prpt`. The PRD's report design will look similar to the following screenshot:

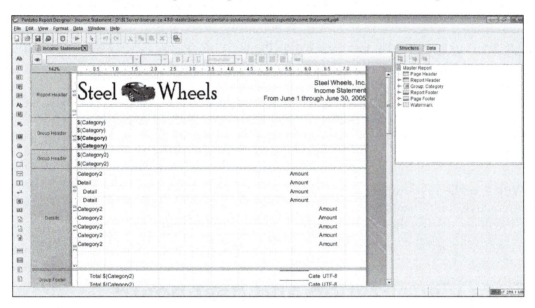

4. The designer layout consists of a pull-down list and a menu bar at the top, a component toolbox in the left-hand pane, the workspace in the center, layout structures and data connection in the upper-right pane, and a properties window in the lower-right pane.

5. Explore the data source using the **Data** tab in the upper-right pane. It contains two data sources:

   ○ **SampleData**: This is a relational query data source with a JDBC connection.

   ○ **Table**: This is a static list of values. It will be used as a report parameter.

6. Within the workspace, click on any item available, whether it is an image, a label, or a field. Click on the **Structure** tab on the upper-right (the tree-like structure) and properties of the item show up.

7. On the **View** menu, choose **Preview**. It will display the report filled in with data. Close the view by toggling on the same menu again.

If you design a report and want to publish it directly to BI Server, you can do it by going to the **File** menu and selecting the **Publish** option. The prerequisite for this is that you needed to have edited the [BISERVER]/pentaho-solutions/publisher_config.xml file and typed in a password. If you leave the password field blank, you cannot publish the report.

Specify your password as pentaho inside the publisher-password XML node and then restart the BI Server.

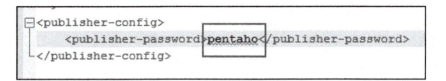

With Pentaho Reporting's capabilities and flexibilities, we can also put more interactive components on the report page. Since, PRD is a big topic in itself, we will not discuss the tool any further. For more information on PRD, see http://goo.gl/gCFcdz and http://goo.gl/HZE580.

Data visualization and dashboard building

Before we begin discussing dashboard designer tools, it is best to clarify that only Pentaho EE has a preconfigured package to create a dashboard using an easy and user-friendly wizard with predefined templates and official support. Fortunately, there is an open source equivalent available—CTools. CTools is an additional plugin from Webdetails. Pentaho acquired Webdetails in 2013.

The following components are the parts of CTools that we will use:

- **CDF**: This is a development framework for building a user-friendly dashboard layout and design

- **Community Data Access (CDA)**: This is a data connector to various data sources, and has a caching mechanism

- **CDE**: This is a web editor plugin that simplifies the process of creating dashboards based on CTools components
- **Community Chart Components** (CCC): This is a JavaScript charting library that acts as a visualization toolkit

CDE has the ability to create static or highly interactive chart components based on a layout template that we can design in a flexible way. We can easily install the tools from Pentaho Marketplace (see *Chapter 2*, *Setting Up the Ground*, for more information on Pentaho Marketplace).

To work on CDE, we need to understand its three architecture layers, given in the following list:

- **Layout**: This is the HTML code to provide a base for the layout rendering of the dashboard.
- **Components**: These are items or widgets to display the data that comes from a data source
- **Data Sources**: These are data providers for the components. They can query data from relational databases, OLAP engines, or text files.

The following diagram shows the architecture layers of CDE's dashboard:

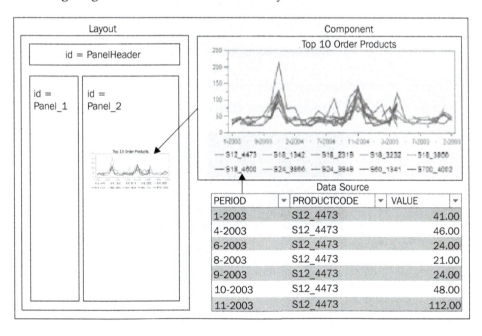

In order to use CDE, you will need to have enough proficiency in HTML JavaScript, and CSS. These are important skill sets required to build the CTools dashboard.

Creating a layout using a predefined template

Use the following steps to create a layout using a predefined template:

1. Launch PUC.

2. Click on the **New CDE Dashboard** icon in the PUC menu bar as shown in the following screenshot:

3. A new dashboard page editor appears. There you can see the **Layout**, **Component**, and data source menu bar items along with a few pull-down menus to manage your dashboard file. Click on **Layout**; it will be highlighted as shown in the following screenshot:

4. The layout editor appears; it has two panes: **Layout Structure** and **Properties**.

5. Above the **Layout Structure** pane, click on the **Apply Template** icon.

6. In the template chooser dialog, select **Filter Template** and click on the **OK** button. Click on **OK** again in a confirmation dialog. The following screenshot shows the template chooser wizard dialog:

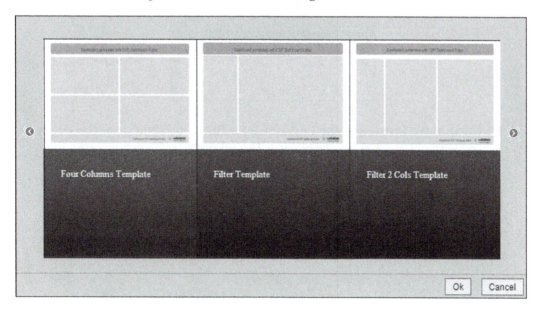

7. In seconds, CDE populates the layout structure with the **Row**, **Column**, and **Html** type items organized in a tree layout structure. Every item will have names that correlate to their HTML DOM IDs.

8. Click on **Preview** in the menu bar. You should get a warning telling you to save the dashboard first. This is a straightforward message and the only one that CDE can render. A preview of the dashboard will only be available once there is a CDE file stored in the solution folder.

9. Fill in the following values, click on the **Save** menu item, and then click on the **OK** button:

   ° **Folder**: Chapter 4

   ° **File Name**: sales_order_dashboard

   ° **Title**: Sales Order Dashboard

   ° **Description**: Leave this field blank

10. Refresh the repository cache. In a moment, the dashboard name shows up in the **Files** pane. The following screenshot shows the dashboard name we specified — **Sales Order Dashboard** — displayed in the **Files** pane:

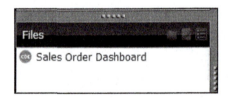

11. Click on the **Preview** menu in your CDE editor. You should see the simple, predefined layout of the dashboard. The following screenshot shows the IDs of layout's part. We will later use these IDs as placeholder identifiers for our components.

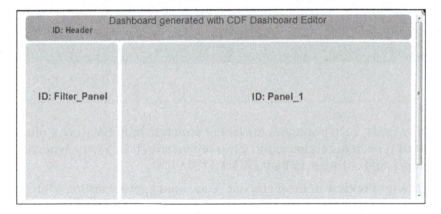

12. Close the preview by clicking on the **X** button. The default title of the dashboard is **Dashboard generated with CDF Dashboard Editor**.

13. Expand the first node of the **Layout Structure** pane, that is, the node with the **Header** ID.

14. Expand the **Column** type node, which is a direct child node of the **Row** type.

15. Click on the **Html** node with the name of title.

16. Find the HTML property in the **Properties** pane list. Click on the **edit (...)** button.

17. Change the HTML content using the following code:

```
<h2 style="color:#fff;margin-top: 20px;">Sales Order
Dashboard</h2>
```

18. Click on the **OK** button.

19. See the change by previewing the dashboard again.

Creating a data source

The following steps will help you create a data source:

1. In the CDE editor, click on the **Data Sources** menu.

2. You will see three panels here: **Datasources**, **Properties**, and a panel with a list of data source types.

3. We will add a SQL query from one of the types. Click on **SQL Queries** and select **sql over sqlJndi**. Note that one query item is added to a group in the **Datasources** pane. The following screenshot shows the **sql over sqlJndi** item in the **Datasources** list

4. Fill in the properties of the item with the following values. Note that for **Jndi**, you should wait a while for the autocomplete listbox to show up. Press any arrow key to make the list show up if it does not.

   ○ **Name**: top_10_overall_orders

   ○ **Jndi**: SampleData

   ○ **Query**:

```
SELECT
CONCAT(CONCAT(O1.MONTH_ID,'-'), O1.YEAR_ID) as Period
, O1.PRODUCTCODE
, SUM(O1.QUANTITYORDERED) as Value
FROM ORDERFACT O1
JOIN
(
SELECT SUM(T.QUANTITYORDERED), T.PRODUCTCODE FROM
ORDERFACT
T GROUP BY T.PRODUCTCODE ORDER BY
```

```
SUM(T.QUANTITYORDERED) DESC LIMIT 10
) O2
ON O1.PRODUCTCODE = O2.PRODUCTCODE
GROUP BY O1.PRODUCTCODE, O1.YEAR_ID, O1.MONTH_ID
ORDER BY O1.PRODUCTCODE, O1.YEAR_ID, O1.MONTH_ID
```

We will use this SQL query later as data for our line chart component. The output of the required three fields should be in this order: series, categories, and value.

5. Save the dashboard.

6. Refresh the repository cache. Note that there is a new item in the **Files** pane: **sales_order_dashboard.cda**. The following screenshot shows the new CDE and CDA items created and displayed in the **Files** pane:

7. Double-click on **sales_order_dashboard.cda** to open the CDA solution item. From the listbox, select **DataAccess ID: top_10_overall_orders**. In a moment, CDA will preview the data in tabular format. The following screenshot shows a CDA data preview:

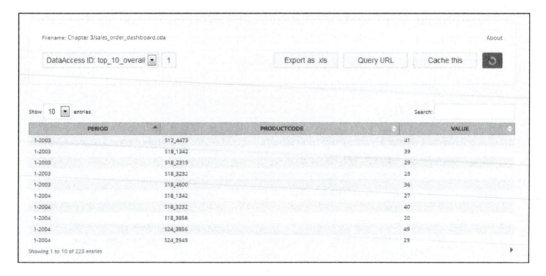

8. Close the CDA and click on the dashboard editing tab to continue working on creating a component in our dashboard.

Creating a component

The following steps will help you create a component:

1. Click on the **Components** menu in the CDE editor.

2. You will see three panels here: **Components**, **Properties**, and a list of available component groupings.

3. From the **Charts** grouping, click on **CCC Line Chart**. It will add **CCC Line Chart** to the **Components** pane. The following screenshot shows the **CCC Line Chart** component:

4. In the **Properties** pane, fill in the following values:
   ° **Name**: top_10_overall_orders_chart
   ° **Title**: Top 10 Orders
   ° **Datasource**: top_10_overall_orders
   ° **Width**: 300
   ° **Height**: 500
   ° **HtmlObject**: Panel_1
   ° **crosstabMode**: False

Note that **HtmlObject** refers to **Panel_1**, which is a right-hand side pane placeholder in our layout.

5. Click on the **Preview** menu. You should see an animated line chart rendered on the right-hand side of the dashboard. The display looks similar to the following screenshot:

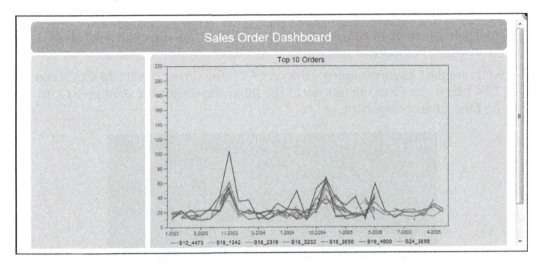

6. Close the preview.
7. Open the CDE menu item directly for the same dashboard to show up.

Summary

We discussed the different stages involved in the business analytics life cycle and how Pentaho provides powerful tools to address analytics challenges with freedom of choice. We also briefly explored some of Pentaho's tools, such as Action Sequence, Report Designer, and CTools.

Performing the tasks described in this chapter will make you familiar with the working environment of Pentaho BI Server and prepare you for the next step—constructing more complex visualization components.

5
Visualization of Big Data

This chapter provides a basic understanding of visualizations and examples to analyze the patterns using various charts based on Hive data.

In this chapter, we will cover the following topics:

- Evolution of data visualization and its classification
- Data source preparation
- Consumption of HDFS-based data through HiveQL
- Preparation of various charts
- Beautification of the charts using styling

Data visualization

Data visualization is nothing but a representation of your data in graphical form. For example, assume you run your data analytics plan and get an enriched data set, which needs to be further studied to extract patterns. In spite of you putting your filtered analyzed data into tabular form with a sorting feature, it would be very difficult to find out the pattern and trend. Even more difficult is to share the findings with the community in case you spot it. Because the human visual cortex dominates our perception, representing data in the form of a picture would accelerate the identification of hidden data patterns.

So, an easy alternative is to represent the data in a graphical manner in terms of charts, which will give a better aesthetic view as well as functionality. This data visualization will communicate information in a crisp, clear, and concise manner. Ideal visualization should not only communicate the information efficiently, but also arouse the viewer's engagement and attention.

Data visualization is associated with information, statistics, and science. In fact, it would be interesting to look at the evolution of data visualization.

The following diagram shows the data visualization journey:

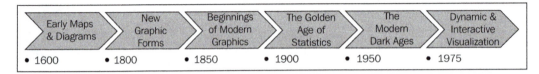

The origin of data representation evolved from geometric diagrams, in the form of celestial bodies such as stars, and in the making of maps to aid in navigation and exploration. The 18th century saw further growth in this field while humanity was starving for navigation, surveying, and territory expansion. A contour diagram was used for the first time in this period.

In the first half of the 19th century, the world saw a lot of inventions in statistical theories initiated by Gauss and Laplace along with huge industrialization. In the anticipation of a pressing need to represent growing numerical information; in the 20th century, the data visualization unfolded into a mature, rich, and multidisciplinary research area. A lot of software tools were made available with data visualization, which was the first dynamic and highly interactive multidimensional data.

KPI Library has developed *A Periodic Table of Visualization Methods*, which includes the following six types of data visualization methods:

- **Data visualization**: This is a visual representation of numeric data in schematic drawing (typically with axes). Examples for this type are pie and bar charts.

- **Information visualization**: This makes use of the visual representation of data—computer supported and interactive in nature—to magnify cognition. It is independent of computers and may involve senses other than seeing, such as sound and touch. Examples are data flow diagrams and Venn diagrams.

- **Concept visualization**: This is a visual representation to exhibit generally qualitative concepts, plans, ideas, and analysis. Examples are mind maps and Vee diagrams.

- **Strategy visualization**: This is the systematic use of complemented visual representations in strategic analyses, development, conceptualization, communication, and the implementation of various strategies in organizations. An example for this type is a life cycle diagram.

- **Metaphor visualization**: This is a visual metaphor showing information graphically in the form of real-life representations to organize and structure information. This metaphor also represents deep insight through the key characteristics of metaphor that are employed. An example of this type is a funnel.

- **Compound visualization**: This is the hybrid use of various graphic representation formats to represent a single schema. An example is a cartoon.

Data source preparation

Throughout the chapter, we will be working with CTools further to build a more interactive dashboard. We will use the nyse_stocks data (please refer to *Appendix B, Hadoop Setup*, for more details), but need to change its structure. The data source for the dashboard will be a PDI transformation.

Repopulating the nyse_stocks Hive table

Execute the following steps:

1. Launch Spoon.

2. Open the nyse_stock_transfer.ktr file from the chapter's code folder.

3. Move NYSE-2000-2001.tsv.gz within the same folder with the transformation file.

4. Run the transformation until it is finished. This process will produce the NYSE-2000-2001-convert.tsv.gz file.

5. Launch your web browser and open Sandbox using the address http://192.168.1.122:8000.

6. On the menu bar, choose the **File Browser** menu.

7. The **File Browser** window appears; click on the **Upload Button**, and choose **Files**. Navigate to your NYSE-2000-2001-convert.tsv.gz file and wait until the uploading process finishes.

8. On the menu bar, choose the **HCatalog** menu.

9. In the submenu bar, click on the **Tables** menu. From here, drop the existing nyse_stocks table.

10. On the left-hand side pane, click on the **Create a new table from a file** link.

11. In the **Table Name** textbox, type nyse_stocks.

12. Click on the NYSE-2000-2001-convert.tsv.gz file. If the file does not exist, make sure you navigate to the right user or name path.

13. On the **Create a new table from a file** page, accept all the options and click on the **Create Table** button.

14. Once it is finished, the page redirects to **HCatalog Table List**. Click on the **Browse Data** button next to `nyse_stocks`. Make sure the `month` and `year` columns are now available.

In *Chapter 2, Setting Up the Ground*, we learned that Action Sequence can execute any step in PDI script. However, since it needs to list the step's metadata using the `getMetaData` method in the `PreparedStatement` class, it will become problematic for a Hive connection. It is because Hive JDBC does not implement the `getMetaData` method. Therefore, we need to work out another way by using Java code that utilizes the `Statement` class instead of `PreparedStatement` in PDI's user-defined Java class.

Pentaho's data source integration

Execute the following steps:

1. Launch Spoon.

2. Open `hive_java_query.ktr` from the chapter's code folder. This transformation acts as our data.

3. The transformation consists of several steps, but the most important are three initial steps:

    ○ **Generate Rows**: Its function is to generate a data row and trigger the execution of the next sequence of steps, which are **Get Variable** and **User Defined Java Class**

    ○ **Get Variable**: This enables the transformation to identify a variable and converted into a row field with its value

    ○ **User Defined Java Class**: This contains a Java code to query Hive data

4. Double-click on the **User Defined Java Class** step. The code begins with importing all the required Java packages, followed by the `processRow()` method. The code is actually a query to the Hive database using JDBC objects. What makes it different is the following code:

```
ResultSet res = stmt.executeQuery(sql);
while (res.next()) {
  get(Fields.Out, "period").setValue(rowd, res.getString(3)
  + "-" + res.getString(4));
  get(Fields.Out, "stock_price_close").setValue(rowd,
  res.getDouble(1));
  putRow(data.outputRowMeta, rowd);
}
```

The code will execute a SQL query statement to Hive. The result will be iterated and filled in the PDI's output rows. Column **1** of the result will be reproduced as `stock_price_close`. The concatenation of columns **3** and **4** of the result becomes **period**.

5. In the **User Defined Java Class** step, click on the **Preview this transformation** menu. It may take a few minutes because of the MapReduce process and because it is a single-node Hadoop cluster. You will have better performance when adding more nodes to achieve an optimum cluster setup. You will see a data preview like the following screenshot:

Examine preview data			
Rows of step: User Defined Java Class (18 rows)			
#	stock	period	stock_price_close
1	ARM	2000-7	15.7
2	ARM	2000-8	17.6
3	ARM	2000-9	15.6
4	ARM	2000-10	15.6
5	ARM	2000-11	14.4

Consuming PDI as a CDA data source

To consume data through CTools, use **Community Data Access (CDA)** as it is the standard data access layer. CDA is able to connect to several sources including a Pentaho Data Integration transformation.

The following steps will help you create a CDA data sources consuming PDI transformation:

1. Copy the `Chapter 5` folder from your book's code bundle folder into `[BISERVER]/pentaho-solutions`.

2. Launch PUC.

3. In the **Browser Panel** window, you should see a newly added folder, **Chapter 5**. If it does not appear, in the **Tools** menu, click on **Refresh** and select **Repository Cache**.

4. In the PUC **Browser Panel** window, right-click on **NYSE Stock Price – Hive** and choose **Edit**.

5. Using the same procedure described in *Chapter 4, Pentaho Business Analytics Tools*, create the following three data sources:

Name	line_chart_data	pie_chart_data
Kettle Transformation File	hive_java_query.ktr	hive_java_query.ktr
Query (represents a step)	line_chart_data	pie_chart_data
Variables (1)	stock_param_data (Arg), STOCK (Value)	stock_param_data (Arg), STOCK (Value)
Parameters (1)	stock_param_data (Name), ALLSTOCKS (value)	stock_param_data (Name), ALLSTOCKS (value)

The variables and parameters in the data sources will be used later to interact with the dashboard's filter. The `Variables` textbox allows more than one pair. And `Variables(1)` indicates that it is the first index value of the `Arg` and `Value` pair. The same explanation goes to `Parameters(1)`.

6. In the **Browser Panel** window, double-click on stock_price_dashboard_hive.cda inside **Chapter 5** to open a CDA data browser. The listbox contains data source names that we have created before; choose **DataAccess ID: line_trend_data** to preview its data. It will show a table with three columns (stock_symbol, period, and stock_price_close) and one parameter, stock_param_data, with a default value, ALLSTOCKS. Explore all the other data sources to gain a better understanding when working with the next examples.

Visualizing data using CTools

After we prepare Pentaho Data Integration transformation as a data source, let us move further to develop data visualizations using CTools. See *Chapter 4, Pentaho Business Analytics Tools* for the introduction of the tool.

Visualizing trends using a line chart

The following steps will help you create a line chart using a PDI data source:

1. In the PUC **Browser Panel** window, right-click on **NYSE Stock Price – Hive** and choose **Edit**; the CDE editor appears. In the menu bar, click on the **Layout** menu. Explore the layout of this dashboard. Its structure can be represented by the following diagram:

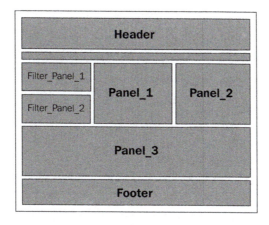

2. Using the same procedure to create a line chart component described in *Chapter 4*, *Pentaho Business Analytics Tools*, type in the values for the following line chart's properties:

   ○ **Name**: ccc_line_chart

   ○ **Title**: Average Close Price Trend

   ○ **Datasource**: line_trend_data

   ○ **Height**: 300

   ○ **HtmlObject**: Panel_1

   ○ **seriesInRows**: False

3. In the menu bar, click on **Save**.

4. In the **Browser Panel** window, double-click on the **NYSE Stock Price – Hive** menu to open the dashboard page.

Interactivity using a parameter

The following steps will help you create a stock parameter and link it to the chart component and data source:

1. Open the CDE editor again and click on the **Components** menu.

2. In the left-hand side panel, click on **Generic** and choose the **Simple Parameter** component.

3. Now, a parameter component is added to the components group. Click on it and type stock_param in the **Name** property.

4. In the left-hand side panel, click on **Select** and choose the **Select Component** component. Type in the values for the following properties:

   ○ **Name**: `select_stock`

   ○ **Parameter**: `stock_param`

   ○ **HtmlObject**: `Filter_Panel_1`

   ○ **Values array**:
   ```
   ["ALLSTOCKS","ALLSTOCKS"],
   ["ARM","ARM"],["BBX","BBX"],
   ["DAI","DAI"],["ROS","ROS"]
   ```

To insert values in the **Values array** textbox, you need to create several pair values. To add a new pair, click on the textbox and a dialog will appear. Then click on the **Add** button to create a new pair of **Arg** and **Value** textboxes and type in the values as stated in this step. The dialog entries will look like the following screenshot:

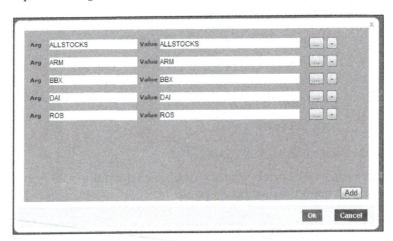

5. On the same editor page, select **ccc_line_chart** and click on the **Parameters** property. A parameter dialog appears; click on the **Add** button to create the first index of a parameter pair. Type in `stock_param_data` and `stock_param` in the **Arg** and **Value** textboxes, respectively. This will link the global `stock_param` parameter with the data source's `stock_param_data` parameter. We have specified the parameter in the previous walkthroughs.

6. While still on editing section of **ccc_line_chart**, click on **Listeners**. In the listbox, choose **stock_param** and click on the **OK** button to accept it. This configuration will reload the chart if the value of the **stock_param** parameter changes.

7. Open the **NYSE Stock Price – Hive** dashboard page again. Now you have a filter that interacts well with the line chart data, as shown in the following screenshot:

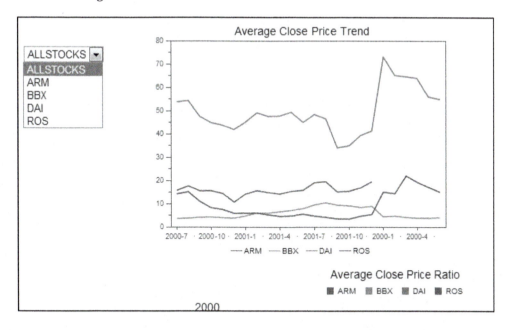

Multiple pie charts

A pie chart is useful to show the contribution of some categories compared to the total. The following steps will show how you can create a multiple categories chart using CDE:

1. Open the CDE editor.

2. In the left panel, click on **Charts** and choose the **CCC Pie Chart** component. The component shows up in a group. Click on it and then in the **Properties** box, click on **Advanced Properties** and type in the value for the chart's properties:

    ○ **Name:** ccc_pie_chart

    ○ **Title:** Average Close Price Comparison

    ○ **Listener:** ['stock_param']

    ○ **Parameter:** ["stock_param_data","stock_param"]

    ○ **Datasource:** pie_chart_data

    ○ **Height:** 300

    ○ **HtmlObject:** Panel_3

  ° **MultiChartIndexes**: `["0"]`

  ° **seriesInRows**: `False`

 MultiChartIndexes is the important property that determines the multiple pie chart divisions. In this example, the index is zero, which means that the first column of the data (**year**) will be a division property.

3. Open the **NYSE Stock Price – Hive** dashboard page. Now, you have a multiple pie chart based on year categories. Try to use the existing filter against the chart. Have a look at the following screenshot:

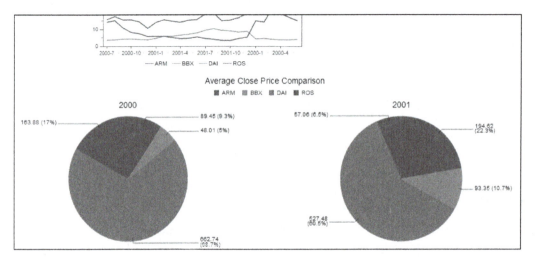

Waterfall charts

Waterfall is a type of chart that can compare data proportionally between categories and subcategories. It provides a compact alternative to a pie chart. Indeed, we will use the same data source that renders our pie chart.

The following steps will help you create a waterfall chart:

1. Open the CDE editor page of the dashboard and click on the **Components** menu.

2. In the left-hand side panel, click on **Charts** and choose the **CCC Pie Chart** component. The component shows up in a group. Click on it and then in the **Properties** box, click on **Advanced Properties** and type in the values for the chart's properties:

  ° **Name**: `ccc_waterfall_chart`

- ○ **Title**: Average Close Price Proportion
- ○ **Listener**: ['stock_param']
- ○ **Parameter**: ["stock_param_data","stock_param"]
- ○ **Datasource**: pie_chart_data
- ○ **Height**: 300
- ○ **HtmlObject**: Panel_2
- ○ **crossTabMode**: False
- ○ **seriesInRows**: False

3. Open the **NYSE Stock Price – Hive** dashboard page. Now, you have a waterfall chart based on year categories differentiated by stack colors. The following chart also clearly shows the breakdown of a stock's average close price proportion:

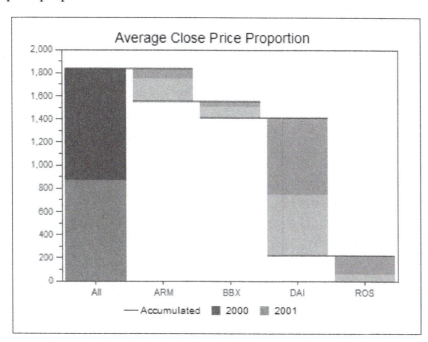

Move your mouse cursor over the top of the leftmost bar chart's area; you should see an accumulated sum of all the stocks' average close price for a particular year. It also shows a proportional percentage.

Then move to a breakdown chart, and you should see a particular stock's average close price for a year, and the percentage of its contribution as shown in the following screenshot:

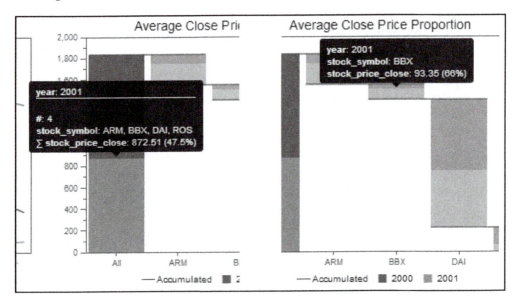

CSS styling

If you feel that the current dashboard's look and feel is not so good, you can improve them through the CSS styling. The CDE editor has an embedded editor that lets you code in CSS without an additional tool.

The following steps will help you use the embedded editor to change the dashboard's look and feel:

1. In the CDE editor, click on the **Layout** menu.

2. Now click on the **Add Resource** icon in the layout structure panel.

3. The pop-up dialog appears, choose **CSS**, then **External File** and click on the **OK** button.

4. Type in the following values:

   ° **Name:** Chapter 5

   ° **Resource File:** chapter5addition.css (click on the arrow button and choose the Chapter 5 folder, then click on the **OK** button and type in the value)

   ° **Type:** Css

5. Click on the **edit (...)** button next to the **Resource file** textbox, and an embedded editor dialog appears.

6. Type the following CSS text in the editor and click on the **Save** button:

```
#Filter_Panel_1 {
  width: 100%;
  background: url(down_arrow_select.png) no-repeat right
  #fff;
  border: 5px transparent #ccc;
}

#Filter_Panel_1 select {
  width: 100%;
  color: #00508b;
  overflow: hidden;
  -webkit-appearance: none;
  background: transparent;
  border: 2px solid #68c6ed;
}
```

Note that every ID in the layout also becomes an identifier for the CSS style. The code will render the listbox in Filter_Panel_1 with a custom color and down arrow. The following diagram shows the filter listbox before and after the CSS styling:

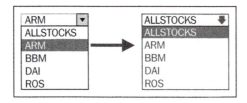

7. Open your dashboard and you should see the final look and feel of the dashboard something like in the following screenshot:

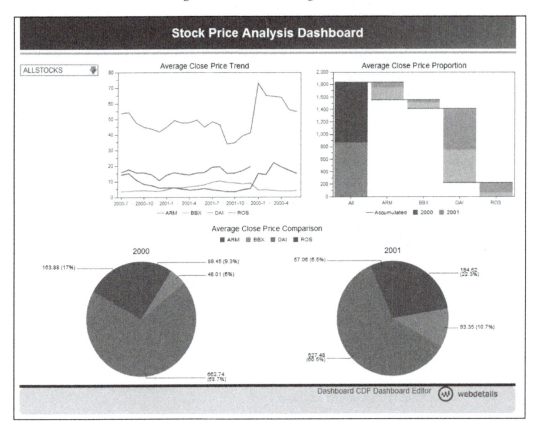

Summary

This chapter showed you how to create an interactive analytical dashboard that consumes data from Hive.

There are numerous types of chart and widget components provided by CTools. However, in this chapter, we focused on building a dashboard using three types of charts (line, pie, and waterfall) to demonstrate the various and essential ways of feeding data to each component. In the latter part, we showed you how to style the page in CDE using the embedded CSS editor.

For more information on the CTools components, go to `http://www.webdetails.pt/ctools.html`. Moreover, if you are interested in CTools samples that are related to Hadoop and Hive, visit our website regularly at `http://download.bigdataclass.com/ctools-samples`.

By completing this chapter, you have acquired the basic skills to work with Pentaho and Hadoop, and are ready to move to a larger scale of Hadoop cluster. Good luck!

A
Big Data Sets

If you really want to check out the real power of Big Data solutions based on the **Hadoop Distributed File System (HDFS)**, you will have to choose the right set of data. If you analyze files of merely a few KBs on this platform, it will take much more time than the conventional database systems. As data keeps growing in GBs and TBs and there are enough nodes in the cluster, you will start seeing the real benefit of HDFS-based solutions.

Data preparation is an important step in a Big Data solution where you have to harmonize various data sources by integrating them seamlessly, using appropriate ETL methodology to ensure that this integrated data can be easily analyzed by a Big Data solution. If you are well aware of the data, you can identify the patterns easily by discovering the data.

Now, the challenge would be to get the Big Data sample from a public domain without any copyright issues. If you have your own large dataset, you are a lucky person. If you don't have such data, no need to curse your luck; there are many such gigantic datasets available in the public sphere with a variety of data, such as that found in social media, science and research, government, the private sector, and so on. Although it's easy to find such sites hosting free data from Google or Quora, for quick reference, this book will share a few links for sites hosting these public datasets. Please do not forget to read the usage terms carefully before using each source just to avoid any infringements.

Freebase

Freebase is a collection of datasets collected from CrowdSource. At the time of writing this book, the size of the data dump in Freebase has reached 88 GB. Freebase is a part of Google.

Visit the Freebase website at https://developers.google.com/freebase/data. For the terms and conditions of the services, visit https://developers.google.com/freebase/terms.

Freebase uses a Turtle data format from **Resource Description Framework (RDF)**, a Semantic Web metadata standard.

For more information on RDF, visit http://www.rdfabout.com/intro/.

U.S. airline on-time performance

The U.S. Department of Transportation's Bureau of Transportation Statistics regularly publishes an *Airline On-Time Statistics and Delay Causes* report on its website. With 29 variables and 123 million rows between the years 1987 and 2008, this dataset may be suitable for you to learn how to handle Big Data.

To download the data, visit http://stat-computing.org/dataexpo/2009/the-data.html. It is originally collected from http://www.transtats.bts.gov.

Amazon public data sets

If you have a hosting account on an **Amazon Web Service (AWS)** such as Amazon **Elastic MapReduce (EMR)**, you can use large public datasets provided freely by Amazon.

At the time of writing this book, there are 54 public datasets available, including human genome data, the U.S. census, the Freebase data dump, a material safety data sheet, and so on. You may find that some of the data sets are too huge to download. For example, the 1000 Genomes Project data size is about 200 TB.

For more information, visit http://aws.amazon.com/datasets.

B
Hadoop Setup

Hortonworks Sandbox

Hortonworks Sandbox is a Hadoop learning and development environment that runs as a virtual machine. It is a widely accepted way to learn Hadoop as it comes with most of latest stack of applications of **Hortonworks Data Platform (HDP)**.

We have used Hortonworks Sandbox throughout the book. At the time of this writing, the latest version of the sandbox is 1.3.

Setting up the Hortonworks Sandbox

The following steps will help you set up Hortonworks Sandbox:

1. Download the Oracle VirtualBox installer from `https://www.virtualbox.org`.

2. Launch the installer and accept all the default options.

3. Download the Hortonworks Sandbox virtual image for VirtualBox, located at `http://hortonworks.com/products/hortonworks-sandbox`. At the time of writing, `Hortonworks+Sandbox+1.3+VirtualBox+RC6.ova` is the latest image available.

4. Launch the Oracle VirtualBox application.

5. In the **File** menu, choose **Import Appliance**.

6. The **Import Virtual Appliance** dialog will appear; click on the **Open Appliance...** button and navigate to the image file.

7. Click on the **Next** button.

8. Accept the default settings and click on the **Import** button.

9. On the image list, you will find Hortonworks Sandbox 1.3. The following screenshot shows the Hortonworks Sandbox in an image listbox:

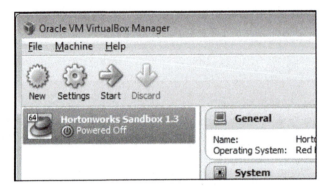

10. On the menu bar, click on **Settings**.

11. The settings dialog appears. On the left-hand side panel of the dialog, choose **Network**.

12. In the **Adapter 1** menu tab, make sure the checkbox labeled **Enable Network Adapter** is checked.

13. In the **Attached to** listbox, select **Bridged Adapter**. This configuration makes the VM as it is having its own NIC card and IP address. Click on **OK** to accept the configuration. The following screenshot shows the VirtualBox network configuration display:

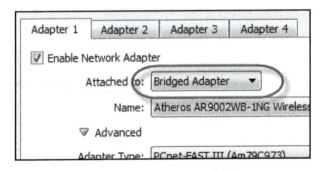

14. In the menu bar, click on the **Start** button to run the VM.

15. After the VM completely starts up, press *Alt + F5* to log in to the virtual machine. Use `root` as username and `hadoop` as password.

16. The sandbox uses DHCP to obtain its IP address. Assuming you can configure your PC to the `192.168.1.x` network address, we will change the Sandbox's IP address to the static `192.168.1.122` address by editing the `/etc/sysconfig/network-scripts/ifcfg-eth0` file. Use the following values:
    - ° **DEVICE**: `eth0`
    - ° **TYPE**: `Ethernet`
    - ° **ONBOOT**: `yes`
    - ° **NM_CONTROLLED**: `yes`
    - ° **BOOTPROTO**: `static`
    - ° **IPADDR**: `192.168.1.122`
    - ° **NETMASK**: `255.255.255.0`
    - ° **DEFROUTE**: `yes`
    - ° **PEERDNS**: `no`
    - ° **PEERROUTES**: `yes`
    - ° **IPV4_FAILURE_FATAL**: `yes`
    - ° **IPV6INIT**: `no`
    - ° **NAME**: `System eth0`

17. Restart the network by issuing the `service network restart` command.

18. From the host, try to ping the new IP address. If successful, we are good to move to the next preparation.

Hortonworks Sandbox web administration

The following steps will make you aware of web-based administration:

1. Launch your web browser from the host. In the address bar, type in `http://192.168.1.122:8888`. It will open up the sandbox home page, which consists of an application menu, administrative menu, and a collection of written and video tutorials.

2. Under the **Use the Sandbox** box, click on the **Start** button. This will open Hue—an open source UI application for Apache Hadoop. The following screenshot shows the Hortonworks Sandbox web page display:

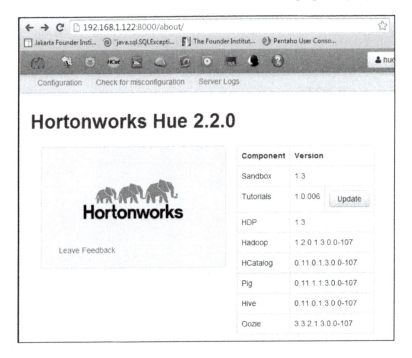

3. On the upper-right corner of the page, note that you are currently logged in as **hue**. The following screenshot shows **hue** as the current logged in user.

4. In the menu bar, explore the list of Hadoop application menus. The following screenshot shows a list of Hadoop-related application menus:

Transferring a file using secure FTP

The following steps will help you transfer a file using a secure FTP:

1. Download the FileZilla installer from `https://filezilla-project.org/`. FileZilla is an open source FTP client that supports a secure FTP connection.

2. Launch the installer and accept all the default options.

3. Now, launch the FileZilla application.

4. In the **File** menu, click on **Site Manager**.

5. When the **Site Manager** dialog appears, click on the **New Site** button. This will create a new site entry; type in `hortonworks` as its name.

6. In the **Host** textbox, type `192.168.1.122` as the destination host. Leave the **Port** textbox empty.

7. In the **Protocol** listbox, select **SFTP – SSH** as the file transfer protocol.

8. In the **User** textbox, type `root`, and in the **Password** textbox, type `hadoop`. Please note that all the entries are case sensitive.

9. Click on the **Connect** button to close the dialog, which in turn starts an FTP session at the destination host.

10. Once connected, you can transfer files between the localhost and the VM. In *Chapter 3, Churning Big Data with Pentaho*, we downloaded `core-site.xml` using this mechanism. We can also download the file from one of these locations: `/usr/lib/hadoop/conf` or `/etc/hadoop/conf.empty /core-site.xml`. The following screenshot shows a FileZilla SFTP session:

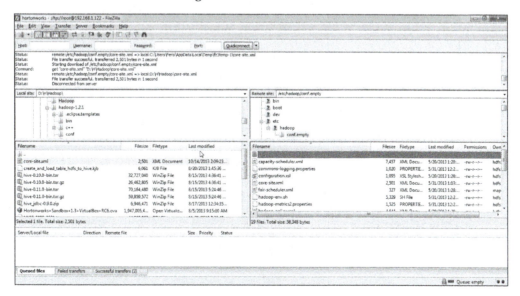

Preparing Hive data

The following steps will make you aware of web based administration:

1. Launch your web browser, and in the address bar, type `http://192.168.1.122:8888` to launch a Hortonworks Sandbox home page.

2. In the menu bar, click on the **HCatalog** menu.

3. In the **Actions** menu, click on the **Create a new table from a file** link.

4. In the **Table Name** textbox, type `price_history`.

5. Leave the **Description** textbox blank.

6. Click on the **Choose a file** button next to the **Input File** textbox.

7. When the **Choose a file** dialog appears, click on the **Upload a file** button. Navigate to the `product-price-history.tsv.gz` file—no need to extract it—and click on **Open**. Once the upload process finishes, the file will appear in the listbox. Now, click on the filename to close the dialog.

8. You may need to wait a few moments before the HCatalog automatically detects the file structure based on its content. It also shows a data preview in the lower part of the page. Note that it automatically detects all the column names from the first line of the file. The following screenshot shows the **HCatalog Data Preview** page display:

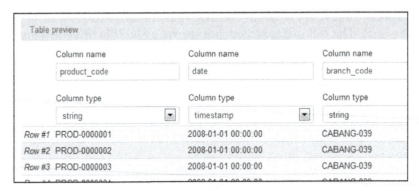

9. Click on the **Create Table** button; the Hive import data begins immediately.

10. The **HCatalog Table List** page appears; note that the `price_history` table is updated in the list. Click on the **Browse** button next to the table name to explore the data.

11. In the menu bar, click on the **Beeswax (Hive UI)** menu.

12. A **Query Editor** page appears; type the following query and click on the **Execute** button.

```
Select * from price_history;
```

Shortly, you will see the query result in a tabular view.

While you are executing the query, until it finishes, the left panel displays a box with the **MR JOB** (MapReduce Job) identifier. It indicates that every SQL-like query in Hive is actually a transparent Hadoop MapReduce process.

The identifier format will be in `job_yyyyMMddhhmm_sequence`. Now, when you click on the link, the job browser page appears and should look similar to the following screenshot:

13. Now, we will drop this table from Hive. In the menu bar, choose the **HCatalog** menu. The **HCatalog Table List** page appears; make sure the checkbox labeled **price_history** is checked.

14. Click on the **Drop** button. In the confirmation dialog, click on **Yes**. It drops the table immediately. The following screenshot shows you how to drop a table using HCatalog:

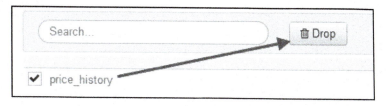

The `price_history` table consists of 45,019 rows of data. In *Chapter 3, Churning Big Data with Pentaho,* we will show you how to use Pentaho Data Integration to generate and populate the same data.

The nyse_stocks sample data

The data sample `nyse_stocks` is from Hortonworks Sandbox. Since we are using the sample data in some parts of the book, download and install the data file located at `https://s3.amazonaws.com/hw-sandbox/tutorial1/NYSE-2000-2001.tsv.gz`.

If you need a step-by-step guide on how to set it up, see `http://hortonworks.com/hadoop-tutorial/hello-world-an-introduction-to-hadoop-hcatalog-hive-and-pig/`.

Index

JRE_HOME 15

M

Mahout 39
management layer, Hadoop ecosystem
  Chukwa 40
  Elastic MapReduce (EMR) 40
  Flume 40
  Oozie 40
  ZooKeeper 40
MapR-FS 39
message template 21
Metadata Editor tool 11
metaphor visualization method 75
MultiChartIndexes 82
MultiDimensional eXpressions (MDX) 11

N

Natural language processing (NLP) 58
nyse_stocks sample data 98

O

OLAP (Online Analytical Processing) 20
Oozie 40

P

Parameters property 80
PDI
  about 42
  Big Data plugin, setting up 42, 43
Pentaho
  about 7
  history 7, 8
Pentaho Action Sequence
  about 19
  creating, Pentaho Design Studio used 19
  JPivot 20
  message template 21
Pentaho Administration Console (PAC) 10,
    27, 28
Pentaho Analyzer tool 10
Pentaho BI Server
  about 13
  JAVA_HOME 15

JRE_HOME 15
Pentaho Administration Console (PAC) 13
Pentaho Marketplace 25
Pentaho User Console (PUC) 13
running 16
system requirements 14
Pentaho BI Suite
  components 8, 9
Pentaho BI Suite, components
  data 9
  design tools 11
  server applications 10
  Thin client tools 10
Pentaho CE
  about 13
  obtaining 14, 15
Pentaho Community Edition. See Pentaho
    CE
Pentaho Dashboard Designer (EE) tool 10
Pentaho Data Integration. See PDI
Pentaho Design Studio 19
Pentaho EE 13
Pentaho Enterprise Console (PEC) 10
Pentaho Enterprise Edition. See Pentaho EE
Pentaho Interactive Reporting tool 10
Pentaho Marketplace
  about 25
  used, for Saiku installation 25-27
Pentaho Report Designer. See PRD
Pentaho User Console (PUC)
  about 10
  Browse pane 19
  Repository Browser 19
  running 17, 19
  working space, components 18
Pig 39
PRD 61-64
Predictive analysis 58
Predictive Modeling Markup Language
  (PMML) 58

Q

quartz 25

R

Report Designer tool 11

Thank you for buying
Pentaho for Big Data Analytics

About Packt Publishing

Packt, pronounced 'packed', published its first book "*Mastering phpMyAdmin for Effective MySQL Management*" in April 2004 and subsequently continued to specialize in publishing highly focused books on specific technologies and solutions.

Our books and publications share the experiences of your fellow IT professionals in adapting and customizing today's systems, applications, and frameworks. Our solution based books give you the knowledge and power to customize the software and technologies you're using to get the job done. Packt books are more specific and less general than the IT books you have seen in the past. Our unique business model allows us to bring you more focused information, giving you more of what you need to know, and less of what you don't.

Packt is a modern, yet unique publishing company, which focuses on producing quality, cutting-edge books for communities of developers, administrators, and newbies alike. For more information, please visit our website: www.packtpub.com.

About Packt Open Source

In 2010, Packt launched two new brands, Packt Open Source and Packt Enterprise, in order to continue its focus on specialization. This book is part of the Packt Open Source brand, home to books published on software built around Open Source licences, and offering information to anybody from advanced developers to budding web designers. The Open Source brand also runs Packt's Open Source Royalty Scheme, by which Packt gives a royalty to each Open Source project about whose software a book is sold.

Writing for Packt

We welcome all inquiries from people who are interested in authoring. Book proposals should be sent to author@packtpub.com. If your book idea is still at an early stage and you would like to discuss it first before writing a formal book proposal, contact us; one of our commissioning editors will get in touch with you.

We're not just looking for published authors; if you have strong technical skills but no writing experience, our experienced editors can help you develop a writing career, or simply get some additional reward for your expertise.

Pentaho Data Integration 4 Cookbook

ISBN: 978-1-84951-524-5   Paperback: 352 pages

Over 70 recipes to solve ETL problems using Pentaho Kettle

1. Manipulate your data by exploring, transforming, validating, integrating, and more

2. Work with all kinds of data sources such as databases, plain files, and XML structures among others

3. Use Kettle in integration with other components of the Pentaho Business Intelligence Suite

Pentaho 3.2 Data Integration: Beginner's Guide

ISBN: 978-1-84719-954-6   Paperback: 492 pages

Explore, transform, validate, and integrate your data with ease

1. Get started with Pentaho Data Integration from scratch

2. Enrich your data transformation operations by embedding Java and JavaScript code in PDI transformations

3. Create a simple but complete Datamart Project that will cover all key features of PDI

Please check **www.PacktPub.com** for information on our titles